meeting management

Speech Communication Series

meeting management

Henry L. Ewbank, Jr.
Purdue University

WM. C. BROWN COMPANY PUBLISHERS, *Dubuque, Iowa*

SPEECH SERIES

Consulting Editor

BAXTER M. GEETING, PH.D.
Sacramento State College
Sacramento, California

Copyright © 1968 by
Wm. C. Brown Company Publishers

Library of Congress Catalog Card Number: 68-24360

Printed in U. S. A.

Dynamic developments of our time, particularly the communication explosion and new revelations concerning human behavior, demand fresh approaches to the teaching of speech. Modern life places an emphasis on speech as an *act of communication,* interdisciplinary in nature, capable of adding new dimensions to man's evolution and progress in all areas of life. The SPEECH COMMUNICATION SERIES, addressed to the introductory student, represents a significant attempt to provide new materials for today's teaching needs.

Basic to all titles in the series is the desire to present the material in the clearest and most lucid style for the purpose of making speech communication a useful, ethical and satisfying experience. While the individual titles are self-contained, collectively they provide the substance for a comprehensive study of those topics fundamental to a basic course in speech communication.

INTRODUCTION

The essence of meeting management lies in three principles as relevant to simple conversational etiquette as to the most intricate and formal parliamentary code. The meeting that will (a) maintain respect for the rights of each individual, (b) agree to abide by the will of the majority, and (c) focus on one idea at a time will invariably accomplish the most in the least possible time.

Procedure appropriate to any specific meeting is determined by the mixture of four factors: the size of the group, the extent to which members agree or disagree, their knowledge of traditional forms and formalities, and the goal or purpose of the meeting. As any one of these four factors changes — from meeting to meeting or within the same meeting — the procedure should change to adapt to the new situation.

Simple listing of general principles is not enough to assure comfortable and effective participation in meetings. This book will start you on the road to understanding and appreciation of how, when, and where those principles will be applied and observed. The rest of the way will depend on your own participation and observation as a member and as a leader in effective meeting management.

The first chapter describes three situations, differing widely in size, member agreement, formality and goals. These are *Meetings: for Better and for Worse*. With these as examples, Chapter 2 sets forth some determinants of *When to Hold a Meeting*. Once committed to a meeting, it is necessary to consider *Participating in a Meeting* (Chapter 3), and *Serving a Meeting as Leader* (Chapter 4). Because the manner of proceeding differs between the smaller, less formal, committee-type meetings and the larger, more formal business meetings, it is necessary to explore *Parliamentary Practice in Committees* (Chapter 5) and *Parliamentary Practice in Business Meetings* (Chapter 6). *Everyday Parliamentary Motions* (Chapter 7) and *Other Useful Motions* (Chapter 8) need detailed explanation and description so that participants are familiar with them and feel comfortable as they are used. A knowledge of *Organizational and Procedural Structure* (Chapter 9) is important to understand the framework of our organizations that hold meetings. Appropriate ways and means of meeting management are discussed, in summary, as *Strategy in Meeting Management* (Chapter 10). *Learning Meeting Management* (Chapter 11) suggests ways of increasing confidence and competence in participation and leadership through individual observation and study as well as classroom practice.

As in any presentation of parliamentary procedure, a quick-review summary chart of the important motions is included, in the hope that it will be referred to only after the main body of the text has been read. It is no substitute for understanding the rationale that determines the important characteristics of the motions. It will seldom be needed by those who know the fundamental principles of meeting management.

CONTENTS

Chapter 1

MEETINGS: FOR BETTER AND FOR WORSE

The work of managing a meeting varies in degree, but not in kind, no matter how large or how small, how simple or how complex, the meeting is to be. Meeting management begins with the decision to call a number of people together and carries through to the completion of whatever business is transacted.

The stories of three meetings widely spaced along the range of size, member agreement, formality, and goals will provide a basis for exploring the principles and factors that affect the achievement and satisfaction of those who participate in meetings.

When Mamie Glotz, president of the Happy Valley Garden Club, felt the need for authorization to spend $22.57 from the club's treasury to take advantage of the special mail order offer on gladiolus corms, she called together the Executive Committee. Their constitution provided that a special meeting of the club could be called by a majority vote of the Executive Committee, comprised of the officers and two members-at-large. By asking these other ladies to come to her house at 1:30, just after the children returned to school, Mamie was setting the wheels in motion to meet this immediate need. Because both she and her fellow officers were busy as homemakers and as active citizens of the community, she had given them ample warning and let them know that there was a real justification for the meeting so that it would take precedence over competing demands on their time. She did provide a bit of social facilitation by serving coffee and dessert, which did not unduly prolong the meeting, but might have offended three of the ladies who were counting calories.

At 1:45, when Carla Tanner, Secretary, had not yet arrived and all of the others (except Beth Orlan, member-at-large, who told Mamie that she had a conflicting dental appointment of long standing) were starting their second cup of coffee, Mamie called Carla's home to see if she had forgotten that this was the Thursday of the Executive Committee meeting. Carla was completely nonplussed by the call. She had her minutes ready and waiting to be picked up in the front hall, but her watch had stopped. So she replied that she would arrive in five minutes if the rest of the ladies would please disregard the fact that she was wearing slacks because she had been in the process of spreading peat moss around her junipers. In the meanwhile, the other officers became just a little concerned over the passage of time, and decided to steer the conversation toward its original purpose so that the meeting would not be prolonged beyond 3:10 when their children would be out of school and returning to homes where there was no parent present. Thus, the Executive Committee meeting really began without being formally called to order as the ladies, by a sort of common consent, began to consider the topic that had provided the reason for their coming together.

Marge Lamb, Treasurer of the Garden Club and conscientious guardian of a safe margin in the checking account, asked Mamie for some of the details of her proposal to spend club funds. What sort of place was selling the corms? Where had Mamie seen the ad? How many glads would they get for the price? Was there fair assurance that they would grow? In turn, Marge was asked whether or not there was a sufficient balance to meet this unforeseen expense. Rose Leaman wanted to know where the glads would be planted, or how they would be distributed. Was this purchase to be for the benefit of members only, or were they to put the flowers in a public park as a part of the civic beautification project? When Carla arrived, her main concern was whether or not a special meeting had to be called, because it would be up to her to notify all of the members. Perhaps, she suggested, the question could be discussed at the next regular meeting. Vice-President Winnie Montague expressed her concern about finding a place to meet on short notice, but when Marge said that she was sure that the social hall at her church would be available, Winnie's problem was solved.

All of these questions were raised because one member or another felt the answers to be important to her decision in voting on the proposal to call a special meeting of the organization. It did not take long to answer the question about the need for the special meeting, because Mamie showed the ad from one of the country's oldest dealers in seeds, plants, and trees to the rest of the ladies, noting particularly that the last day to place orders was within ten days, and the next regular meeting was not scheduled for three weeks. The constitution was clear, also, and three of the officers had brought along copies because they had had the time and the forethought to get out their copies and look at them. Only the question of adequate funds and distribution of the plantings remained. Marge had prepared a brief summary of the financial holdings and commitments of the club, showing that the $22.57 would be well within the "miscellaneous" category that had been established when the budget had been approved three months earlier. That left the question of what to do with the glads, if they were purchased. Rose Leaman, Chairman of the Civic Beautification Committee (a standing committee of the club) and member-at-large of the Executive Committee, reported that she had been able to contact the members of her committee by phone and they were all agreed that if this special purchase were made, they would furnish the labor for planting in the city park as a part of their continuing program. As Rose completed her report, Winnie suddenly reached for her copy of the constitution, flipped over to the By-Laws section, and scanned it hurriedly. Thus reassured, she stated that if the Executive Committee adopted a motion approving the purchase as a part of the civic beautification project they could avoid calling the special meeting because they were charged with administering this project. They would then simply report their action to the next regular meeting of the entire club. This action made everyone happy, so the motion was formally offered and adopted. The purchase was authorized. No special meeting was necessary. And the rules of the organization were obeyed.

Because each of the Executive Committee members was given ample previous notice of the time and topic for the meeting, much of the necessary thinking had gone on before they got together. Essential questions had been defined and answers secured. Thus these ladies were able to complete their business without delay and return to other matters that required their attention.

In another city the president of the Marmaduke Manufacturing Corporation, makers of electronic components for complex automated systems, was confronted by the third letter in as many days complaining about delays in delivery of the M-43 model. Just as the ladies were departing for home, John Munch (Marmaduke president) called in the Vice-President, Terry Conrad, to ask that he call a meeting of all (and only) supervisors whose departments were involved in any way with the M-43 model in order to discover all possible causes of delay and to decide how these causes could be eliminated. Terry told his secretary to notify the heads of the Sales, Engineering, Production, Shipping, Materials, Accounting, and Quality Control Departments to meet in the Vice-President's conference room in thirty minutes. She did not know why, and he neglected to tell her, so it was simply a "Be there" message without explanation. This led to fears about what the Boss had on his mind and made the men arrive prepared to defend themselves and their department against whatever was to come.

The conference room was designed and furnished for just such a meeting. The table and chairs, chalkboard, scratch paper and pencils, ashtrays, and other paraphernalia were properly set for the meeting. Each of the men responded to the directive to appear on time, leaving unfinished business in his department, because the word came down from above that a conference was to take place. Just after the last man arrived, the Vice-President entered the room and opened the meeting by saying "Somewhere, one of you men, or maybe each of you, is not getting the job done. The Boss has had three complaints that the M-43 is not being delivered on schedule. We have just fifty minutes to find out where the trouble is, so let's get at it."

The response was immediate. Tom Maberly (Sales) said, "We've given the plant two days more than Production said they needed, just as a cushion. It certainly isn't our fault that the orders aren't being filled on time. Haven't things been going all right on the line, Joe?" "We've met every production quota all along the line, Tom," Joe Hillman (Production) replied. "Somebody else is goofing up. Not my boys." "If you're inferring that the Shipping Department isn't getting the M-43's out, you're just dead wrong, Joe," said Jim Cobb, the Shipping Supervisor. "We've had every one of them in the cartons and on the trucks within four hours of the time it came from the line. Believe me, they must be getting held up somewhere else."

I'd say that it was our department," volunteered Tony Glenn, Materials Supervisor, "because we have a lot of trouble getting the materials to meet those specifications. I've sweat bullets a time or two when we were all out of the right weight steel, but we've managed to get some just a day or two before the next orders came through every time, so we're not the problem." "There's nothing wrong with the specifications or the jigs. They're designed just as plainly as they were for the old M-28, and we haven't had the first gripe from anyone who's worked on it," said Eric Busch, the Chief Engineer. "Before I wind up with everyone pointing his finger at me," Mack Snell (Accounting) said, "just let me say I'm not quite sure why I'm here in the first place. We handle these orders just like all the rest, and you guys all ignore Accounting anyway. It's just left up to us to catch up and keep up as best we can, while you jump the gun and get things put together and on the truck." "Well," Quality Control Supervisor Dick Clark said, "If we can believe everyone here, it's nobody's fault, and the customers must just be complaining for something to do. Quality control certainly hasn't been slowing things down. One or two partially assembled

M-43's have had to be sent back for a touch-up, but that's our job. If the circuits aren't right they don't work even if they are delivered, and then the customer really has something to get mad at. I wish I'd known what this meeting was all about, and maybe been given a little more time to get ready for it. My records will bear me out. They're not quite complete up to quitting time last night, but I could have them ready in about an hour, and I'm sure that they will show you I'm right."

Mr. Conrad just sat and looked at his men. Here he was, with a meeting on his hands that certainly had a well-defined purpose, a carefully chosen group brought together because they all were instrumental in creating the problem, and because at least one of them would be involved in working out the solution. True, he hadn't given them much notice, and he hadn't told them what the meeting was about, so none of them had been able to prepare any information or even gather thoughts to bring along. Now each one of them had publicly stated that the problem did not lie with him or his department. At that moment, the prospects for achieving the purpose of the meeting within the time limits established seemed very poor.

Later that same day, in still a third city, the 150 delegates (three from each state) to the annual meeting of the National Council on Education were called to order in the Parliament Room of the Stelz Plaza Hotel, as the chairman, Dr. Martin Darrow, tapped his gavel three times and said, "The Council will please be in order."

Each of the delegates was elected by his State Council for a three-year term, so arranged that one member was elected from each state each year as his predecessor retired. This meant that one-third of the delegates were attending their first meeting, while another third were attending their last. Officers of the Council were elected from among the delegates and retained their membership on the Council, *ex officio*, after their three-year terms expired, retaining voice but no vote except for certain types of business. The yearly election voted one person into the position of Second Vice-President, from which he proceeded automatically through the office of First Vice-President and President in successive years. An Executive Secretary was employed by the Council on a continuing basis as a full-time staff person.

It was Dr. Darrow's sixth consecutive meeting, then, over which he was to preside, and the last one that he would attend unless he happened to be re-elected from his state. He had worked carefully with his Agenda Committee and had outlined the order of business, scheduling reports from standing committees and providing some time for discussion of each before the call for new business which would precede the scheduled

adjournment at 4:30 P.M. two days later. Resolutions previously submitted by the delegates to the Resolutions Committee had been drawn
up in proper form and were ready for distribution in writing to the
delegates when the committee report was called for.

This would be a formal meeting — in several senses of the word.
It would be formal because the number of delegates was large, and
they were not only unfamiliar with each other, but one of every three
was unfamiliar with the traditions of Council meetings. It would be
formal because much of the discussion on resolutions and recommendations had already taken place in the committees; it remained only
for the organization as a whole to review the committee recommendations and adopt them. It would be formal because of the ornate
surroundings, the necessity to use floor microphones connected to the
public address system in order to be heard, and the necessity for each
speaker to identify himself each time he spoke so that the tape re-
cordings of the proceedings would be complete and accurate. And
finally, it would be formal because discussion on each item would be
limited to a total of twenty minutes, with each speaker limited to a
maximum of five minutes at any one time (to be recognized a second
time only after others who might want to speak had spoken). The
parliamentarian who sat at Dr. Darrow's right would help to enforce
these time limits and advise him in the event of any variations from
the correct rules of procedure.

Each of these meetings, widely different from the other in terms of
the number of people involved, physical surroundings, purposes, and
any number of other characteristics that might be named, was closely
related to the other in the rules of behavior that guide the actions of
every participant, from the chairman to the person who is present but
says nothing during the entire meeting.

The development of skill and facility in managing meetings is largely
a matter of experience. Management of meetings means learning to
work effectively with people, and this comes through associating with
them, "getting to know them," observing them work together, and
knowing what to look for.

As we watch people work together, it is imperative to know some
of the factors that affect the manner in which people and ideas interact
with each other. In this way we can learn to distinguish between factors
that always operate, no matter what we do, and those other factors
over which we can exercise some control, thereby making group en-
deavor more or less difficult. By making intelligent choices, where
choices are possible, we can definitely establish better, higher prob-
abilities that our meetings will become much more satisfactory to

everyone concerned: the participants, the chairmen, and those who depend upon the meetings for constructive results.

Chapter 2 provides direction for observation, practice and study to augment the remainder of this book, both for the "do-it-yourself" individual and the member of a class dealing in part or entirely with effective meeting management. Immediate and continuing efforts to establish relationships between description and theory on the one hand, and observation and practice on the other will reinforce the text presentation.

Chapter 2

WHEN TO HOLD
A MEETING

Any time is a good time **not** to hold a meeting.

The only time to hold a meeting is when more than one person is necessary to accomplish the job that must be done. If Mamie had had the authority to make her purchase for the club simply by signing the order herself, there would have been no need even to call a meeting of her Executive Committee. If Terry Conrad had known just where the delay was in the process of manufacturing and delivering the M-43 model, he could have told the President and issued the speed-up order to the proper department without consulting all of the supervisors involved. Finally, if the National Council on Education were constitutionally established to act entirely through committees there would have been no reason for the 150 delegates to meet together to affirm the recommendations of the committees in order to make the actions official in the name of the Council.

When only one person can do or must do the job, there is no reason to — and every reason not to — hold a meeting. And at the same time, if there is no job to be done — no purpose for a meeting — there is real reason not to meet. The first step in meeting management, then, is:

MEET WITH A PURPOSE — A JOB TO BE DONE!

Every person who calls a meeting must see a purpose for himself and for every person whom he asks to attend that meeting. Every person who accepts an invitation to attend a meeting, or who voluntarily appears at a meeting time and place, must have a purpose in mind. One of the most important factors in the story of the rather efficient meeting of Mamie's Garden Club Executive Committee was that she recognized a purpose — a need for all of the Committee members to meet — and she was able to communicate that purpose to each of the others. When they arrived, they knew what had to be done, and they had a common purpose from the start. Because she told them the purpose of the meeting as she invited them to attend they had time to think about what they were to do. And each one had a standard by which to judge the success or failure of the meeting. Indeed, because they had been able to think about Mamie's problem for a while, they succeeded in accomplishing the purpose even more efficiently than she had originally foreseen.

Contrast that meeting with the gathering of the Marmaduke supervisors. Mr. Conrad had a purpose of his own and he had a reason for calling on each other member of the group, but he did not provide a well-defined purpose for those whom he asked to attend. As a consequence, each supervisor arrived with his own purpose — to discover what the Vice-President wanted — but this purpose was only enough to bring him to the room. When Mr. Conrad told them *his* purpose not one of them was prepared to offer constructive suggestions to accomplish that purpose. Each took up a defense against the implied criticism of his department, indicating that his purpose was to shift blame away from himself. Before any real progress could be made toward achieving the primary goal of that meeting — reducing delays in delivery of the M-43 model — Mr. Conrad found that it was necessary to develop a new and different purpose in each member of his group.

People, being as they are, seldom act to accomplish only one purpose at a time. And because meetings of groups involve several people, they involve a range and variety of purposes. The important factor in any meeting, then, is to make sure that the participants agree on the relative importance of the several purposes possible in any given meeting and that the group goals and their individual purposes are assigned the proper priorities. When this occurs it is probable that everyone will achieve the greatest possible satisfaction from the meeting, because each participant judges the meeting against the criteria suggested by the purposes which moved him to attend the meeting. If, for example, the National Council on Education delegate from Indiana attended the Council meeting with the primary purpose of talking with one of the delegates from Idaho, his estimate of the success or failure of the entire conference will be colored by the satisfaction achieved in talking with this one person.

One obvious way to promote agreement on the purposes of a meeting is to declare what those purposes are as the meeting is called. When the meeting is to be relatively formal this is achieved through the publication of an agenda — a list of items in the order in which they will come before the group. With an informal group this is less necessary, but it is no less desirable to supply an answer to the immediate questions which arise in the mind of each person who receives a notice of a meeting, either in writing or by word of mouth: "Why meet? What are we going to do at the meeting?" One thing is certain: if the person who calls the meeting does not supply an answer to these questions, each individual who is attending will supply his own. It then becomes necessary, as it did with the Marmaduke men, to satisfy or replace that individual purpose before a new purpose can be granted top priority.

The determination of a purpose, or of a group of related and ranked purposes, for a meeting will not only establish the need for the meeting and provide motivation for participants to attend, but it will be a highly significant consideration in deciding who should be notified of the meeting and asked to attend. This constitutes the second step in meeting management:

MEET WITH ALL (AND ONLY) THOSE NECESSARY TO DO THE JOB

When either more or less people are involved in a meeting than are directly concerned with its purpose, the group is usually frustrated in its attempts to get the job done. If Mamie had called a special meeting of the entire Garden Club, more time would have gone into the planning of the meeting and the meeting itself. It is possible that the purchase would not have been made because of objections raised by some member who did not understand why the special meeting was necessary, unless it was to veto the idea so the officers would not exert too much control over the organization. Had Terry Conrad called in only one or two of the supervisors of departments concerned with the M-43, he might or might not have guessed the right ones; had he called in every supervisor in the plant, some of them would rightfully ask "Why are we here?" Businesses, under the banner of "efficiency," do try to involve minimum numbers in their meetings so that the number of man-hours devoted to conferences remains as low as possible. This same principle of economy should govern all meetings. It has been said that the complexity of meetings increases as the square of the number attending. With three people involved a meeting has a complexity factor of nine; by adding two more members that factor increases to twenty-five. Whether or not this is literally true, it seems clear both in theory and practice that only those who are necessary should be present at a meeting. It is equally clear that when members who should be present are missing, another meeting of some sort will be necessary. And this becomes a poor economy.

More frequently, perhaps, the problem becomes one of adjusting a job to the existing size of a group. When any continuing group takes up new business, it is confronted with the potential of being the wrong size to get the job done. If the group is too large for efficient handling of a question, it will usually refer the question to a committee comprised of just a few of its members. For example, when it is proposed that the Rotary Club make a special donation of money and volunteer time to paint the South Side Community Center, a committee might well be created to study the alternatives, work out the details of a specific proposal, and submit a recommendation to the entire membership at a later meeting. In this way, by scheduling a series of meetings of small and large groups, the problem can be tailored at several successive stages to the size of the different groups. If it works out that the Rotary Club is not big enough to do the job, they, in turn, may act to involve still others in order to get it done.

To determine the appropriate size of the group which is to meet, it becomes necessary to determine in some detail just what is to be done to accomplish the purpose or purposes to be achieved by those who are to be present at the meeting. This has already been referred to when the agenda for a meeting was mentioned. Thus the third factor of successful meeting management is:

MEET ONLY AFTER PLANS ARE COMPLETE

Each meeting — no matter how large or how small, or what its purpose is — must be preceded by planning. Every meeting ever held could have been improved by better planning.

Time and place of meeting are only two of the important decisions which must be made before a meeting can be held. Each decision affects and is affected by each other planning decision, so there is no universal sequence in meeting planning. Organizational structure, traditions, and commitments automatically decide some of the plans. Regularly scheduled meetings are a part of the structure of many organizations; some have regular meeting places or a pattern of meeting periodically in different locations. At the other end of the line, groups formed temporarily to achieve a given goal have no such patterns to rely on, so the determination of time and place can be crucial. Avoiding conflict with prior commitments of time and securing the best possible surroundings to create the right atmosphere for success are especially vital aspects of planning irregular or occasional meetings.

Meeting planners must anticipate and provide for every foreseeable development. Because "a meeting" might occupy time ranging from a few moments to several days or weeks, the planners must take careful account of the duration of their meeting to assure that the time and goals are adapted to each other. It makes as little sense to schedule a three-day meeting to determine the programs for a series of five meetings of the PTA as it does to try to develop a report on activities of the United Fund organizations in a single forty-five minute meeting. Planners must either fit the duration of the meeting to the pre-established goal, or limit the goal to the time available for the meeting.

In addition to planning for appropriate time, place, and duration for a successful meeting, there may also be specific equipment or accessories which will be necessary or at least convenient to include in meeting plans. Such items as a gavel, a speaker's stand, a table or suitable chair for the secretary, enough chairs for the participants, tables for a committee, a chalkboard (and what good is it without chalk and an eraser?), a slide or movie projector (with a screen or light wall and controllable light in the room), electrical outlets or extension cords, scratch pads and pencils for committee use, ash trays, refreshments available, good ventilation, and controllable temperature suggest the range and scope of the physical considerations which come within the purview of completing plans for your meeting. When plans are properly made such items simply "are there" when needed. They seldom are accorded great comment when they do appear at the appropriate time. But when the progress of the meeting is interrupted because someone wants to use a chalkboard and there is no chalk, or participants can find nothing to doodle or make notes on, these aspects of meeting planning take on inordinate significance. As the participants look back on a very satisfactory meeting, noting points of satisfaction, these details of good planning emerge as important factors. Here, perhaps, is where the science and art of meeting planning meet. Plans can be developed through a scientific analysis of all possible needs of the group and scheduled co-ordination with the agenda items. The effect on the participants will be that of good art, wherein the techniques of achieving the impression do not call attention to themselves, but contribute to the enjoyment and satisfaction.

A final aspect of good planning includes a consideration of what might happen. The chairman who has considered how participants may respond or react to proposals will not be caught on a procedural hook; and the member who has planned alternative courses of action suitable to several possible situations will know how to respond and what to propose in order to achieve his own preferred goals.

Prior consideration of the way to proceed can set the mood for probable success; lack of effective consideration can create probability of failure. Just as a meeting can be interrupted by the lack of needed equipment, progress can be halted by lack of needed assurance that there is a way to do what the participants want done. True, the person who calls the meeting is not the only one who must complete plans before a meeting can be held. He has done the best he can when he anticipates to the best of his ability, knows how to meet whatever he can foresee, and provides time in which the participants can plan in a like manner.

This kind of planning necessarily involves knowledge of how people can be expected to behave in meetings, what factors determine how they behave, and how to structure a meeting situation so that there is the highest probability that people will be satisfied with it. Becoming increasingly better acquainted with the general principles, as well as specific practices of meeting management, is a far more reliable road to success than the hurried reference to a parliamentary authority in a moment of stress while the meeting is in progress.

Having completed plans down to the last foreseeable detail for a meeting with a purpose involving everyone (and only those) necessary to achieve that purpose, there remains but one other preparatory step:

MEET ONLY AFTER EACH MEMBER OF THE GROUP
HAS BEEN NOTIFIED

In part, this rule is just simple courtesy but it may be absolutely necessary when the meeting is not a matter of routine. Every participant deserves to be informed of a meeting in sufficient time to arrange his schedule so that he can attend. Every meeting planned to include all and only those who are necessary to its success deserves to be attended by everyone who is expected. To jeopardize potential success through delayed notification of the participants is to fail in what is usually the easiest step to follow.

Informing the participants of the nature of the business or problems with which the meeting will be concerned is equally important to its success. Only in this way can each member have the time to devote prior thought to his part in the ultimate success of the meeting. As he considers items of business, proposed actions, or questions noted for discussion, he will be able to form an initial viewpoint, and perhaps to gather some information needed to support his position. Even if he arrives at no definite position, the participant can frame some questions which may bring out information leading to decision.

It might be observed that each of the meetings described in Chapter 1 provided for notification of the members. However, the Marmaduke Manufacturing Corporation meeting was a classic example of how *not* to notify participants of a meeting. It failed to provide enough time for each of the supervisors to make adequate provision to attend the meeting. Because each of the men had left behind unfinished work, his mind was still partially occupied with it. This necessarily decreased his ability to participate constructively in the meeting until he became interested and involved. Equally important, the notice of the meeting did not include any hint of its purpose, thus leaving each person to ponder, "What do they want? Who else is going to be in on this one? How long is this session going to take?" Had the supervisors known the problem that would confront them, they could have used some of their thirty minutes to find answers to some such questions as, "What is different about the M-43 model in my department? Can I think of any changes which would speed up the overall production on this model?" Indeed, despite the urgency of the President's demand for action, it is probable, in light of the way the hurry-up meeting got started, that it was headed for failure and the need for a second meeting. This might have been avoided by notifying the supervisors of a time and an agenda for a meeting the following day, giving them enough time to gather thoughts and information so as to arrive ready to attack the problem.

It is impossible to establish just how much advanced warning is necessary or desirable. There are, however, at least two sets of guidelines which will be helpful to meeting planners. First, the desirable amount of advanced notification increases as the duration of the meeting, the distance traveled to attend, and the degree of formality of the meeting increase. A meeting of the National Council on Education, described in Chapter 1, would require an initial notice a matter of months or a year before the opening gavel was to sound. Then, in order to stay within the limits set by the other guideline — namely, a notice should be sent near enough to the meeting time so that it is impossible to forget or to postpone active planning for participation — a follow-up notice, including the agenda, should be sent to all those who are to attend about a month before the meeting is to be held. For meetings lasting only a matter of hours, involving little or no travel from one place to another, only the second type of notice is needed. It should be so timed as to strike a balance between permitting time to arrange schedules easily and to prepare for active participation, and not being so far ahead as to permit anyone to forget.

SUMMARY

When more than one person is necessary to accomplish a goal those involved should

MEET WITH A PURPOSE — A JOB TO BE DONE.

When that purpose is defined it becomes possible to

MEET WITH ALL (AND ONLY) THOSE NECESSARY TO DO THE JOB.

So that the meeting can proceed without unnecessary interruption they should

MEET ONLY AFTER PLANS ARE COMPLETE.

And in order for all participants to arrive fully prepared to contribute to achieving the goal, they should

MEET ONLY AFTER EACH MEMBER OF THE GROUP HAS
BEEN NOTIFIED

Chapter 3

PARTICIPATING
IN A MEETING

It should be accepted as an article of faith that no one simply "attends" a meeting. Everyone, by his physical presence, "participates" in a meeting — more or less actively, to be sure, but the passive connotation of "attending" is neither desirable nor accurate. The person who apparently does nothing but sit during a meeting is, by his very inaction, affecting the participation of others. Some will respond by imitation, others by contributing more than usual, but everyone reacts in some degree to everyone else at a meeting. In fact, one can even "participate" in a meeting through his own absence. Members who are present react to the fact that other members are not there. Those present feel more or less free to participate actively. *Participating* in a meeting, then, concerns the way in which each member affects the course and the outcome of the meeting.

PREPARING

Every participant in every meeting ever held began to prepare for each meeting the day he was born. Because this is true no one can fully "manage" (in the sense of "engineer" or "control") a meeting. Also because every person carries his whole life with him into every meeting he attends, the more successful meeting experiences an individual has had, the more effective his participation is likely to be. Previous meeting experiences with the same group of people, or dealing with the same topic, affects his expectations and the contributions to later meetings. If a chairman has conducted meetings effectively in the past, he is expected to do so again. If Jim Cobb has appeared to be very much on the defensive before, it comes as no surprise when he shows the same attitude again. Another member who has repeatedly missed the point in meetings will be counted on to miss the point again.

Even though people cannot be relied on to be consistent, all of these expectations, hopes, biases, and attitudes make up each person's general preparation for participating in any given meeting.

Specific preparation begins at the moment of receiving advance notice of a particular meeting. At this time the question must be asked, "What is *my* reason for participating in *this* meeting?" When the announcement is made, or the invitation to participate is extended, it should suggest an answer, or several answers to this question. If, as has been suggested, the purposes of the meeting have been determined, and everyone (and only those) necessary to achieve those purposes has been invited to attend, the announcement stating the purpose of the meeting will provide ample answer. "The next regular meeting of the Booster's Club will be on Monday," suggests that this meeting is held to satisfy a constitutional requirement for periodic meetings. Routine business can be expected. If anything out of the ordinary, such as a constitutional amendment, is to be considered, this should be made clear in the announcement. "The organizational meeting of the Sailing Club will be held on November 30," is perfectly clear in its intent. Each of these announcements provides enough information to determine whether or not there is something to gain, to achieve, or to contribute by participating in the meeting.

When one cannot decide that he really has a purpose in participating in the meeting he owes it to himself, and to everyone else in the group, to secure more information about the meeting. In any case, the first step is to find a clear reason or reasons to participate.

Once the reason to attend is clear, the way is paved to make sure that the purpose can be achieved. When it is simply a routine periodic meeting, it may be legitimate to conclude that mere physical presence and an answer to roll call are all that is necessary so that a quorum is present and the regular business can be transacted. It is one of the unfortunate facts of contemporary society that there are so many routine meetings and so little accomplished in the number of man-hours invested in them. Such meetings tend to color the expectations developed for meetings which really should actively involve those who are present, making for passive acceptance of proposals that really deserve thoughtful consideration. If no quorum is present for a routine meeting no business can legally be transacted. Continued failure to attract a quorum should soon force the organization to become more active or to dissolve. Either alternative would be an improvement over the continuation of humdrum gatherings without vital purpose.

But let's assume that there is a more positive reason to participate; that there is a genuine commitment to a purpose that demands some action through meeting with others. When this is the case, active specific preparation is required. The Garden Club Executive Committee members had the opportunity to reread their constitutions and to arrive at some conclusions about how best to proceed. In another instance, if a formal motion to propose a dance were on the agenda, members would be able to decide what facts they needed in order to arrive at an intelligent decision. Initially, each member could take inventory of the knowledge he possessed that would affect his vote: What are other plans in the community? Dates already taken, music available? How does the community react to dancing as compared with other forms of entertainment? What do members of this organization know about the business of sponsoring a dance — costs and popularity of specific bands, sources of information or contacts with such bands, cost of renting adequate facilities for the event, publicity necessary to promote attendance, means and locations of selling tickets, etc.? Whose opinions in the group are the most reliable in making this decision? These questions and others like them will lead to the information necessary to effective participation in a meeting.

Possession of information, or the recognized need for information is not enough to insure effective participation. The ability to secure support from others for a favored point of view or position is equally important. This support can come only through a successful combination of two factors: first, knowledge of the proper procedure for the meeting, and second, ability to present ideas so that other members will understand and accept them — the skill of persuasion.

Through specific preparation for a given meeting — efforts to define reasons for participating in that meeting — each member will discover what he knows from his own past experience, what he must find out from other sources, and how he can contribute his information and ideas appropriately and persuasively. As he thinks through these questions, he will arrive at a positive commitment to participate actively in the meeting and probably he will establish an initial point of view on the business at hand. At the same time, it should be evident that this initial point of view should be tentative, held with the acknowledged possibility that some other member might offer an unconsidered idea that could cause a change of opinion. It is worth noting that no one is really expected to cling to his original position if, through discussion, he is led to some new ideas which make him want to change his mind. Robert A. Taft became one of the most respected legislators of his time precisely because he publicly reversed his position on a number of important national issues as he gained new information and insights. Effective preparation for participation will lead to an initial position or to knowledge of what information is necessary to determine that position. This will lead to a personal commitment to participate in the meeting either by expressing a point of view or by listening actively and raising questions that will elicit the ideas of others. When this commitment has been achieved each member is ready for the meeting to begin.

PERFORMING

Committee chairmen and organization presidents are constantly urged to begin meetings on time, and the best way to co-operate is for each participant to be there ready to start at the appointed hour. Both your preparation for participation and your consideration of the other members become evident when you appear promptly.

Once the meeting is under way, each member makes his greatest contribution to successful meeting management by following the progress of the business. Attention should be focused on the proceedings. Keeping the eyes and ears directed at the chairman, or whoever has the floor, decreases diversion. Side conversations and occasional remarks are not so easily heard. In fact, as all of the participants focus on the discussion, the number of remarks directed at neighbors decreases. Everyone becomes more concerned with being a member of the total group.

There are several benefits in being actively involved in the meeting. One of the basic principles of all group operations is that when things are working right each group will get the most done in the least amount of time. Unnecessary formalities are dropped, routine matters are handled with dispatch, digressions from the points at issue decrease because participants are eager to get the job done, and, most important, the time spent in reviewing what has happened is cut to the minimum because the participants know what is going on.

One way to keep attention focused on the progress of the meeting is to take notes — notes for yourself only, not the same kind that the secretary is taking. This amounts to a sort of doodling with a purpose: jotting down key words or ideas as the discussion proceeds. Such notes will help each member decide when he can contribute to the discussion himself. They will help construct a question or prepare a statement supporting or opposing points previously made. They can also assist in keeping the parliamentary situation clear, no matter how formal or informal the meeting is.

Everything that is said in a meeting falls into one of two categories: questions and statements are either *substantive* (about the *topic* being considered) or *procedural* (about the *manner* in which that topic is being considered). Substantive contributions can be further distinguished on the basis of their purpose. A member can: (1) add information not already brought out by someone else, (2) restate information in order to clarify, emphasize, or summarize what has already been said, (3) ask a question which will bring out new information necessary to an intelligent decision, or (4) express clearly his own point of view indicating how he will vote when the issue is put to the test. Procedural comments are motions or informal suggestions indicating what should be the next step toward decision, or questions that seek advice on how to progress. Unless one of these is the conscious purpose of the speaker, he will probably make a greater contribution to the discussion by listening to others than by indulging his own desire to speak.

Your initial commitment to attend and participate in a meeting should remind you that each member accepts an implied contract as he begins working with groups of people. By your very presence you commit yourself to contribute to the success of the meeting — to help the entire group achieve the goals which they have set for that meeting. This means that each member of a group is under some obligation to assist the leader and the other members by whatever contributions seem to advance the group along its chosen path. On occasion, this may mean, as suggested above, that he will supply information that no one else has brought out or ask the leading question which brings the information from someone else. At any given moment it may be appropriate to draw together a summary of what has been said about a particular point, so the group can determine the necessity of talking further about it. At one time he may try to draw out a comment from someone who has been silent for a long while. At another he may seek to quiet an over-talkative participant.

The theorists list each of the contributions above as leadership functions, but this does not mean that only the leader should perform them. Indeed, if this were so, the leader would be the sole performer in the meeting. Nothing would be left for the participants to do. On the contrary, the leader in the formal meeting should simply make it possible for members to state their minds by controlling the traffic of ideas according to rules previously agreed upon. In less formal small group meetings, the leader should look at his own position as being that of ultimately, rather than immediately, responsible for leadership functions. If no one else sees the need to curtail a comment or suggest a transition to a new topic, the leader should move as he sees fit to insure progress. As the group grows better acquainted, the members will determine the functions they can perform to achieve and sustain the appropriate degree of formality or the kind of organization that will work best for their particular group and its problems.

As each meeting draws to a close it is extremely important that each participant be aware that some progress has been made. He should have clearly in mind those agreements which have been reached, how many of the overall goals or objectives have been achieved, what the next steps will be, what his own responsibilities are, and the date, time, and goals of any subsequent meetings. He may then begin his specific preparation for that next meeting and his efforts to achieve the next interim goal in pursuit of the ultimate objective.

SUMMARY

Each participant should make specific preparation for each meeting, and every participant should prepare as if he were going to serve as leader of the meeting, because, in a sense, he does lead as he participates. This means sorting and organizing his information and ideas and filling in the gaps where he lacks the necessary knowledge to develop a point of view. It means determining the initial position that he will hold until and unless he is lead to a new position through new or additional information. It means the determination of a goal that the meeting can be expected to achieve so that he can realize the satisfaction of demonstrable progress achieved during each meeting, though it may take a series of individual meetings to accomplish the adoption of a particular program. And finally, it means following the progress of the discussion so that he knows when and how best to contribute in order to uphold his part of the unwritten contract to work with the others for the common purpose.

Chapter 4

SERVING THE MEETING AS LEADER

For untold generations people have studied leaders to determine just what makes them tick. What makes *him* a leader? Why do people follow him? What does he do to cause others to look to him for leadership? Why can't *I* be a leader? These are all aspects of the same question that has defied a succinct and definitive answer as long as it has been posed. Men's lives have been studied, theories have been developed, books have been written, and in every case the answer has been found in a certain set of circumstances that is different in some respects from all other situations. As a consequence it is impossible to generalize, and when one seeks to emulate a great leader he is doomed to failure because he cannot recreate the same conditions for leadership.

It often happens that the same man who excels in leadership in one type of situation fails woefully in another. The military hero is seldom a great political leader, though he may capture the votes to gain election. U. S. Grant is often cited as an example of the effective military leader who became an ineffective political figure. And so it is that the person who presides effectively over a large formal meeting may be most ineffective as chairman of a small informal committee. The leader must achieve his success in each new situation by meeting the expectations of his prospective followers.

Specific leadership responsibilities in any particular organization are defined by the organization itself, through its rules and traditions. Within these limits, there are some aspects of parliamentary tradition and general etiquette that hold in all democratically oriented groups. Foremost among these is that the leader — be he "president," "chairman," "moderator," "exalted leader," or whatever his title — is the servant of the members. Whatever he does in the name of the group is done in order to advance the purposes of the group, and he is held accountable by the rest of the membership. One remains a leader only so long and so far as he enjoys the confidence of the group which he leads. There are times when a person continues to hold his leadership title after he has lost his effectiveness. This occurs when there are rules or traditions that specify tenure in office. In these instances the real leadership role is being filled by someone else working within the structure, either through the co-operation of the past leader or through by-passing him. If an organization is to continue, the leadership functions must be continuously performed by one or more persons.

Leadership duties and responsibilities in any meeting fall into two definable periods: those that must be performed before (including right up to the very moment) the meeting begins, and those that are carried on during the meeting. Perhaps a third time period — follow-up activities — could be defined, but these can be considered as occurring during the period preceding another meeting.

PREPARING

One significant factor in serving a group successfully as a leader is the preparation that must precede the actual meeting. Much of this preparatory work is identical with that performed by the members. Indeed, successful participation as a member is almost universally seen as a prerequisite to any exercise of leadership. Someone must recognize a leadership potential before asking a person to assume a leader's role. A measure of success in one leadership position almost inevitably leads to later opportunities to undertake larger ventures with greater responsibilities. As the leader studies each situation, he discovers what is similar to his previous meetings, and what, in each instance, makes the meeting unique. It is this analysis and adaptation to each new situation which distinguishes the successful leader.

In addition to his general preparation as a participant in the meeting, the leader notifies the members that a meeting is to be held, signalling the start of the period of specific preparation. As he designates the time, place, and agenda for a meeting, the leader assures the members that these matters have been considered with care. Where a group is large or rather formal, this leadership responsibility may be shared with one or more committees — committees on time and place, and agenda are common. Even when time and place are routine, the leader can contribute greatly to the activity level in his meetings if he avoids the category of "routine" meetings.

The constitutions of an overwhelming number of American organizations specify the frequency and regularity with which members are supposed to meet. It is entirely possible that when a group is being organized everyone sees great need to meet weekly or monthly because enthusiasm and interest are high enough to insure constructive business at every meeting. After a busy organizational period the amount of business may drop, but the frequency of meetings seldom drops with it. This increases the humdrum routine aspects of the meetings, and leaves the members to devise ways to ward off boredom. One of the primary challenges that a leader must prepare to face, after some initial meetings that serve to reassure himself and the members of his leadership abilities, is the challenge of fulfilling members' demand for interest and accomplishment in the regular periodic meetings of the group.

The goal of avoiding "routine" meetings cannot constitutionally be achieved by ignoring the provision that meetings must be held. It is almost always extremely difficult to amend a constitution to reduce the number of meetings. The only alternative, then, is to raise the periodic meetings out of the category of "routine." The leader should plan each meeting to include at least one specific problem which will motivate participation by the members and will create a feeling of achievement as the meeting is adjourned.

Where a group is created to achieve a delegated purpose, such as a committee formed by a larger organization to study a problem or consider a proposal in detail, the leader is the committee chairman, either appointed or elected by his committee. These groups, unless specifically instructed to meet at a particular time and place, meet on call of the chairman, who schedules the meeting and notifies each member so that he can be present. In other situations, when one person has a problem, he becomes the leader with the responsibility not only to call the meeting, but to determine who is to be asked to attend. He must consider carefully who has helpful information or who must co-operate in implementing a solution and invite all who will contribute (and only those who are necessary to get the job done successfully). When the list of those who might contribute to the consideration of the problem grows too large, or appears to include members who do not work well together, the leader should seriously consider the possibilities of establishing one or more subcommittees or subgroups with specific responsibilities to assess a part of the problem and report the results of their discussions. This method increases the number who participate in the decision without increasing the complexity of operations in any group.

In every situation the leader should be well-informed regarding (1) the subject matter of the meeting, (2) those who are to participate in the meeting, and (3) the proper procedure to be followed in conducting the meeting. Indeed, the leader is usually selected or elected because he has more than the usual knowledge of at least one of these aspects of meeting management. It is his responsibility, then, to inform himself concerning the other two.

It may seem unwise to designate the person who is the most knowledgeable in the group and put him in a position where he is compelled to remain neutral or impartial, as a leader is often expected to do. Still, this is often done, and can be defended on one or more of four grounds. First, leader selection on the basis of subject knowledge is very likely to take place as a committee is created, because the person who originates a motion which subsequently is referred to a committee becomes the most likely prospect as its chairman. In the procedural pattern of committees, the chairman is more free to offer opinions and to participate in the discussion than he is in the more formal plenary sessions. Traffic control of discussion in a committee is less difficult, and is usually shared among the members, so one or another of them can keep the chairman from abusing his privilege to speak, thereby dominating the committee.

A second reason for naming the best informed person to the chairmanship of a committee is that he is very likely to be the person most highly motivated to complete the committee investigation, develop the new policy, and get the new program under way. Third, the concentration of knowledge best qualifies a person to perform the leadership functions, insuring that the subject is thoroughly investigated, and of focusing on the most important aspects so that the best use is made of the meeting time spent. Fourth, it can be argued that if someone other than the chairman or leader is recognized as having the most knowledge, a split develops in the leadership with participants turning to one of the members as a subject matter leader and to the chairman for procedural leadership. This situation is not altogether undesirable, provided that the members of the group do not seek to abandon the chairman-leader altogether.

Important as it is for the leader to be well informed concerning the subject matter, it is even more important that he be well informed about the proper procedure for its consideration. He should be sufficiently familiar with the whole range of proper procedure so that he can select and adapt the degree of formality according to the size of his group, the degree of unanimity, the knowledge of procedural rules, and the pressures acting on the group for a quick resolution of the problem.

It is equally important for the leader to be as well acquainted as possible with the members of the group with whom he is to meet. As he determines who should be included in a meeting, he should draw up his list from those who will bring to the meeting the necessary information, ideas, and insights to achieve the goal. Or, to put it another way, he should do all that he can to make sure that those who attend the meeting come prepared with the necessary information, ideas, insights, and commitment to get the job done.

Physical arrangements for the meeting constitute another responsibility of the leader. He must make sure, even before the meeting notices are sent out, that the best available room is reserved. It should be a size which is scaled to the size of the group, set up in the manner (auditorium, face-to-face, etc.) most conducive to establishing the atmosphere desired, furnished with note pads, pencils, and copies of necessary written reports, and adequately lighted and ventilated. Provision should be made in advance for any special equipment, such as chalkboards, projectors and screens, recorders, or easels. In sum, he must anticipate as many of the physical arrangements as possible in order that the forward progress of the meeting not be interrupted.

PERFORMING

Once the members are assembled and the meeting is getting under way, the leader should exert his positive influence to establish and sustain an atmosphere in which the members will help him to help them accomplish their main task. His manner should be assured, because he knows how to conduct the meeting, he knows the basic rationale of good etiquette, group process, and parliamentary procedure, and he is prepared to work with the members according to these patterns in order to get the most done in the least time. The leader's self-assurance in conducting a meeting will, in turn, reassure the members that progress can be and will be made, and that if they are in doubt about the right way to do things, they have but to ask, and the leader can supply the answer.

For his part, the leader's knowledge of principles should assure him that even if he is not clear about a specific rule, as long as he is consistent with the general principles, reflects the sentiments of the majority of the group, and respects minority rights, both he and they are acting within the spirit of parliamentary practice. He can be confident, too, in the knowledge that if he departs from good practice in any ruling, the members have the right and duty to appeal from that decision.

It is the responsibility of the leader to keep the members informed of the current status of the discussion and particularly to make sure that the members have a clear picture of the effect of any votes which they may cast. It is impossible to estimate how much time has been lost and how many people have lost faith in parliamentary rules because they did not understand exactly what they were voting on, or which way to vote in order to express their preference.

Because the management of meetings becomes significantly easier as everyone in the group gains experience and assurance in the procedural patterns, the leader can contribute to the growing effectiveness of the organization by anticipating procedural problems and explaining the proper way to handle them. In some organizations a brief explanation of a rule or a situation, treated as a committee report, is included as a regular part of each meeting. Through the course of a series of meetings this practice will help the members become better informed and will gradually improve the way business is transacted.

As the meeting progresses, the leader must be responsive to the needs and desires of the members. He should make sure that his view of his responsibilities as leader corresponds closely with the expectations of the members. If he starts a meeting with the thought that the group will require strong leadership, and finds that they are capable of progressing without close direction, he should let the members assume more responsibilities. If he expected the group to be capable of moving along well, but sees that they have become bogged down, he will need to increase the amount of direction that he is supplying.

Fundamentally, the basis of effective group process and of good parliamentary procedure is found in the simple principles of good etiquette. What is proper and appropriate when conversing with one or more friends in a social situation is equally proper in the most formal of organizations — the differences are of degree, not kind. Likewise, what is improper in conversation will be equally improper in more formal situations. Just as it is impolite to interrupt and talk over someone else's voice in conversation, so one person only may have the floor at a time in a parliamentary session. Just as it breaks down a conversation to talk about several different ideas at the same time, parliamentary rules provide that there be only one topic or motion under discussion at any time. Just as the most casual conversational decisions in groups are arrived at by a majority agreement that still acknowledges the existence of differences, so the rules of order balance the dominance of majority vote with a respect for minority rights and opinions. The most satisfactory and pleasing conversations develop among those who know fairly well what reaction to expect from each other; in the same way, the best meetings occur when the leader and the members are agreed on their respective roles. As everyone acknowledges that he should:

1. talk about one thing at a time
2. abide by the will of the majority
3. respect the position and rights of the minority,

he will, at the same time, recognize the basic tenets of good etiquette, effective group process, and good parliamentary practice. By acting in accord with these principles at any given moment, the leader and the group will almost inevitably make the proper decision even though they cannot recall a specific rule to apply.

SUMMARY

The leader must recognize that because he carries the greatest share of responsibility the ultimate praise or blame for the outcome of every meeting rests primarily with him. Member satisfaction in a meeting develops only where there is an effective combination of leader and members performing the various functions necessary to successful goal achievement. Blame for falling short of meeting goals is almost always placed on the shoulders of the leader, whether he merits it or not. This added risk is offset, to some degree, by the tendency to focus praise on the leader, more than the members, when their collective efforts result in successfully achieving their goals.

Chapter 5

PARLIAMENTARY PRACTICE IN COMMITTEES

Committees are small groups of people seeking to accomplish a predetermined task, usually assigned to them or assumed by them in the name of a larger group or parent organization. Patterns of American organizations, no matter whether they are social, industrial, or legislative, reveal two general categories of committees: special committees and standing committees.

COMMITTEE FUNCTIONS

Special committees are small groups appointed to accomplish a single defined task or objective. They continue to function only until that job is done and their report is made to the parent organization. When the PTA plans a special program, including entertainment, refreshments, and displays of new educational materials, it might well create a special committee to plan and execute the details of the program. This group would then meet on call of its chairman, decide which of the members should be in charge of each aspect of the program, arrange for whatever assistance was needed to make the physical arrangements, serve the refreshments, etc., see that everything went according to plan, and file a report at the regular meeting following the program. At this point, their report would be received "with thanks," and the committee discharged. Traditionally oriented organizations refer to the special committee as an "*ad hoc*" committee, using the Latin phrase meaning literally "for this." When "this" is done, the committee has no further responsibility.

As procedural patterns have developed, the "*ad hoc*" committee was the original type of committee. When it became apparent in some organizations that they were creating and discharging committees for essentially the same type of jobs, it began to make sense that certain

29

committees be kept in continuous existence because the same sort of problem kept repeating itself. Thus, instead of creating a separate committee for each program during a year, a "standing committee" on programs was formed, to plan and execute all of the programs throughout the year. Only when the last program had been successfully presented did the committee cease to have a function, and then it almost inevitably was followed by another year, and another program series.

The standing committee is a small group which continues to exist in an active or stand-by status because its function is a continuing or a recurrent one. Legislative bodies at all levels have "ways and means" committees (or whatever they actually title them) because the function of considering bills and resolutions dealing with money matters is a continuing one. The semi-social, semi-business organization almost inevitably has its parallel committee, though money matters may be handled through its Executive Committee or Board of Directors. The board of directors in industry is similarly charged with the management of capital and with determination of where the corporation shall allocate its money. Whenever a business matter involves the use of funds or resources it is referred to this committee for special detailed study, possible amendment, and recommendation for action. The organization is thus able to provide for a specialization of effort by those best qualified in different areas of interest in order to evaluate the relative importance of each proposal. After such evaluation the committee reports significant information and ideas leading to its recommendation, urging the parent organization to adopt or reject the proposal. Through this "government by committee" a legislative body, as well as a social-business organization, can accomplish more than it could if each member were to join in the collection of information, assessment of importance, determination of alternatives, and proposal of proper action on every proposal which comes before it.

COMMITTEE CHARACTERISTICS

Because of their small size, committees are more closely related to conversational groups than to formal meetings of organizations. The behavior of committee members, then, is bound more by the usual rules of good etiquette than the rules of Robert's or Jefferson's manual of parliamentary procedure. Herein lies both the strength and the potential weakness of the committee process. Most committee members feel that they know how to behave in everyday conversation, hence they know how to behave in a committee meeting. To a degree this is true. But because the committee and the bull session are so much alike, many people fail to recognize the essential differences. It is these differences which spell the choice between effective and ineffective committee meetings.

There are two significant distinctions between social conversation and the business of a committee. First, the committee meets in order to accomplish a common purpose, while the conversational group has no such purpose. It is true that people gather in order to develop better mutual acquaintance and understanding, and that this constitutes a valid purpose for coming together, but the concern here is primarily for human relations, and is independent of the subject matter of the conversation. Committees are concerned with the subject matter of their discussion and may, in the process of achieving this goal, develop better understanding among the members. Second, and closely related to the first, is the fact that the social group is not responsible to any other group for a report of its actions. The committee, on the other hand, does have an obligation to execute the task assigned by the organization of which it is a part. It must arrive at some decision — even if it is only the decision that no action can be or ought to be taken at the moment. Committee members must make a concerted effort to work together, or else they must request to be reconstituted with different personnel if the task is indeed to be accomplished.

Because of these major distinctions from simple social gatherings, certain of the elements of parliamentary procedure are built into committee procedures. Foremost among these is the obligation to abide by the will of the majority in decisions affecting the procedures or the substantive aspects of the meeting. Equally important is the obligation to respect the rights of each member, no matter whether he is a minority of one or a member of an all but unanimous majority. In sustaining these commitments the committee is no different from the most formal parliamentary body. And by the same token, as the committee holds to these commitments it, like the most formal of organizations, will get the most done in the least amount of time. In practice, this commitment can only be met by following those practices which are common to good etiquette, good group dynamics and human relations, and good parliamentary procedure.

Effective management in committee meetings, then, demands that:

1. Only one person speak at a time.
2. Each person seek to limit his remarks to the one topic at hand — to keep "on the track."
3. Comments be concentrated on ideas and information, not on the personalities of those participating in the meeting.
4. Opportunities be provided for expressing the widest possible variety of points of view, including the provision that as a majority develops

the minority or minorities get a fair hearing until the point of final decision is reached, and that even then such minorities retain the right to express their dissenting views to the parent organization.

5. A leader is acknowledged whose ultimate responsibility it is, together with each of the others in the group, to see that the foregoing practices are followed so that the committee meets its assignment, and that committee actions and decisions are reported to the parent organization.

COMMITTEE TASKS

Committee task assignments, in all but a very limited number of instances, will fall into either one of two broad patterns. First, a committee may be appointed to investigate a problem and to develop from that investigation a policy or plan to be reported to the parent organization with a recommendation for action. Second, a committee may be appointed to investigate the acceptability of one or more proposed courses of action that the parent organization has neither the time nor the immediately available resources to consider as a body, and to report a recommendation to the parent organization for action.

In both of these patterns the committee's major function is to investigate, to probe, to discuss in detail a problem that the parent organization would find difficult or impossible to consider as a body. It is in such situations that the values of a committee become important. Because the committee is smaller than the entire organization, it is easier for it to meet conveniently; it is easier for each member to have both the time and the inclination to express himself; it is easier to question and clarify. Each member is more likely to recognize his own responsibility to be informed and to say what he knows about the subject because there are fewer others to rely upon. Committees are usually composed of people who are interested in the particular task at hand, while larger groups are almost bound to include some who are less well informed and interested than a committee of limited size. A committee is better able to consult outside experts or hold hearings to collect testimony than is a larger organization. This is true both because the time of fewer people is demanded, and because both the expert and the layman will be more at ease if they testify before a small group. Finally, the committee is simply more efficient than the entire organization working together, especially when the number of choices is relatively large. It makes better use of the time and talents of the number of individuals involved. The man-hours devoted to accomplishing the job are more productive.

Inherent in the nature of committee assignments to "investigate and report" is the fact that, with certain strictly limited exceptions, committees lack the authority for final action. Parent organizations find it expedient to use the resources of committee action to get a job done efficiently, but they cannot escape the responsibility of making the final decision if that decision is to be made in the name of the entire organization. In one sense this is a part of the principle of majority rule and minority rights. Parliamentary tradition and law prohibit an organization from delegating its decisions to a minority, except perhaps as an executive board or committee may be empowered to act for an organization during periods between meetings. Even here, such a committee is empowered only to act within predetermined policy, and these acts are subject to review and action at the next periodic meeting. This limitation prescribes the final product of committee action: the report.

COMMITTEE REPORTS

The report of a committee represents its achievement. All of the work of the committee points toward the report which it is to make. As intermediate goals are set and achieved by a committee engaged in investigation of a problem, progress reports can be made so that the parent organization can be kept abreast of developments. In considering problems of any real scope or complexity it is good practice to establish such intermediate goals, both for the morale of the committee and for the assurance of the organization as a whole. Committee members involved in a series of meetings can soon become impatient if they cannot see progress toward their ultimate goal. Even when interim reports are not filed with the appointing body, it is helpful to the committee itself to draw up an account of what has been achieved, where it has been, and where it is going.

This suggests that it is good practice to establish a goal or purpose for each separate committee meeting and to keep minutes to show just how well the purpose of each meeting was achieved. One rather common pattern of goal-setting is to follow the steps of the decision-making process, or "scientific method" suggested by John Dewey and adapted to discussion by numbers of others. Essentially this defines the steps in arriving at a policy decision as follows:

1. Locate and define the problem.
2. Explore the problem.
3. Propose alternative solutions.
4. Select the best solution.
5. Seek the adoption of the best solution.

This program for problem-solving provides a series of interim goals that will help the committee to continue making progress in a given direction and to sustain interest and enthusiasm for a long-term assignment. It will also provide an excellent basis for the end product of the committee efforts — the committee report.

The composition and scope of the committee report is determined by its assignment and by the manner in which the meetings have been managed. If the committee has been asked to investigate a problem and recommend action to the parent organization, it is expected to go successively through all five of the steps of problem-solving. The men's service club (e.g., Rotary, Kiwanis, Optimists) that establishes a "Committee on Juvenile Problems" makes this kind of an assignment. The committee members are expected to gather information from local sources to find out whether or not the community has any "juvenile problems," and if so, what they are. On the basis of these findings, then, they can develop a program which will meet the situation.

When a proposal has been made in a business meeting, and referred to a committee, the job is a bit different. Under the heading of "new business" a member might offer this motion: "Mr. Chairman, I move that the club underwrite rental costs for two months on the Jackson Building to help establish a teen-age recreation center." Here, a proposal that is advanced as the best solution is offered for action, but the organization as a whole does not feel that it has enough information to accept or reject the solution at that time. The function of the committee, then, is to work backwards from this solution to discover what led to its being proposed. Having done so, the committee is in a position to recommend acceptance or rejection of the proposal, or possibly, that the original proposal be modified, or that an alternative should be adopted. In support of any one of these recommendations the committee must present enough evidence to lead other members of the organization who have not made the detailed study to agree with the recommendation. This, of course, is the fifth and final step in the decision-making process.

Throughout the early stages of committee consideration it is most important that the committee operate with as few procedural restrictions as possible in order to focus maximum attention on the subject at hand rather than on the rules under which it is being considered. As a committee develops into a group — in the sociological sense of the word — as the members get to know each other and know that each is dedicated to the same task, only the simple rules of good conversational etiquette are really necessary. The chairman will not need to perform very much of the "traffic cop" function of leadership. He can be relatively free to participate substantively in the discussion. Each member will share in some degree the functions of leadership. Questions may be asked directly, without going through the chairman, and they may be answered directly. The atmosphere will be informal and as permissive of full and free discussion as possible.

As the investigation by the committee becomes complete and the time for decision and reporting arrives, there will be somewhat greater need for a defined formal procedure. Indeed, there is need for a clear and binding procedure at any step when decisions are to be reached. If this is understood by the entire committee, step by step progress can be recorded in the minutes of the meeting. If at any point one of the members wants to review agreements already reached, it is a simple process to review actions taken.

Establishing Agreement

The simplest method of reaching and recording agreement is through common consent. When the chairman feels that substantial agreement has been reached on any issue under discussion, he has only to say, "We seem to have agreed upon. . . . Is there anyone who objects to this statement? May I take it by consent that we put this statement in the minutes?" He should pause a moment here, so that anyone who does not agree really does have a chance to express himself. Especially at the early stages of discussion, it is good practice to record not only the fact that there is disagreement, but to record the gist of the different points of view. There is ample precedent for this, even at the concluding stage of problem solving, in the issuance of decisions in multiple-judge courts, such as the United States Supreme Court. Only in those instances when all of the justices agree not only on the decision, but on the reasons for that decision, is a single decision, written by one of the justices, rendered. When any justice has a view that is not shared by others, he writes his own opinion that may be different either in its reasoning or in its conclusion, or both. Thus it was, for instance, that the famous Dred Scott decision of the Supreme Court was not "a" decision, but rather seven separate concurring decisions, and two dissenting opinions. Chief Justice Taney wrote "the decision." Each of the other justices wrote his own decision expressing his own individual view of the process of arriving at this conclusion.

The practice of making clear in the early stages of discussion that there are different assumptions and different biases can be beneficial in two ways: (1) it establishes an air of mutual respect for differences of opinion, leading to frank and open consideration of the entire problem, and (2) as parallel lines of analysis are given fair treatment there is a continuing testing to discover the better. Such testing often gets lost when there is no opposition. As one line of thought profits from comparison, it gains a more thorough acceptance than if it had been considered alone.

Often, the "common consent" process, even when noting that differences and dissent exist, is the only means necessary to transact the business of a committee. It does provide justification for the committee report; it avoids unnecessary formality. Occasionally, however, the more formal and traditional method of asking for affirmative and negative votes may be more proper because of the preference of the members or because of the manner in which a proposal is put to the committee.

One limitation or liability of the "common consent" procedure should be noted. The question "Unless someone disagrees, we shall. . . ." is a biased question. It presumes unanimous agreement. It puts a degree of social pressure on each person to express his agreement (usually through his silence, sometimes with an affirmative nod of the head, infrequently through an audible expression of agreement), rather than to express opposition. When each side is asked to vote with a show of hands or a voice vote, everyone must make an overt act in order to have his vote acknowledged. When common consent is requested, only the dissenter must make an overt act — that of expressing his opposition and he does not, for a moment, know whether or not anyone else will agree with him. His may be only the first of a unanimous expression of rejection, but for that moment all he knows is that he is a minority of one, and there at least *seems* to be an assumption that the majority will accept the proposed statement. Most people will succumb to the will of the majority (or what is assumed to be a majority) and will not express their individual opposition. It is, of course, impossible to document how many times this reluctance has contributed to the acceptance of a proposal that was, in reality, agreed to only by a minority who happened to be on the side of the chairman who proposed that common consent be given.

For this reason, "common consent" can be abused. The chairman, or a representative of a vocal minority, can knowingly or unwittingly take advantage of a rather timid opposition to engineer acceptance of a proposal over the unexpressed opposition of a majority composed of individuals who feel that each may be alone in his opposition. The only safeguard, obviously, is for each member to make sure that when he feels opposition to a proposal offered for common consent action, he expresses that opposition. At worst, this will avoid a misleading appearance of a unanimous vote. At best, he may be only the first of a previously silent majority which takes heart from the first expression of opposition and adds up its votes to defeat the motion.

As the committee nears completion of its report the chairman should review the actions taken by the committee, making sure that all significant agreements are recorded. When the entire committee is substantially agreed upon the items which should be reported, and the existence of any defined minority has been acknowledged, it is often wise to turn the raw material over to a subcommittee on style to compose the report. Seldom can even five or six people work as well at composing a report as can one or two. The number of man-hours wasted by large groups trying to work out carefully worded reports is phenomenal. By selecting one or two members of the committee who give evidence of being rather skillful with the language, a good start is made on the report. As these subcommittee members work together to compose the report, they must bear in mind the impressions that the committee wants to convey and the audience it is seeking to reach. The successful report will, as in all effective communication, bridge the gap between these two important elements.

Action on Reports

Earlier it was stated that reports could generally be expected to do either one of two jobs — inform or propose action (persuade) — or both. In the first instance, it is proper to label the report "for information only (or for discussion only)," and to propose that the parent organization simply "receive," "accept," or "file" the report. Such action, when voted upon affirmatively by the organization does not bind it in any way to the information contained in a report. It urges no action, therefore no action is necessary on the report, except, perhaps, discharging an *ad hoc* committee. This kind of a report is appropriate when a committee has been charged only with investigating a problem and reporting the information which it finds, or when submitted as an interim or progress report at some stage before a solution may have been proposed or adopted in the committee.

When a report recommends an action — the adoption or rejection of a particular proposal, solution, or course of action — it should be moved that the organization "adopt" the report. An affirmative vote on the motion to "adopt" binds the organization to the recommendation contained in the report without any further action. Reports containing both information and recommendations should be so written that the latter are separate from the former, and separate motions for disposal of the report can be offered by its chairman. Sometimes these sections of the report are offered separately; the information being presented at the proper time for committee reports, and the recommendations being introduced under "old business" or "new business," depending upon which is the more appropriate.

"AS IF IN COMMITTEE"

We have strayed from the story of informal committee procedure to introduce just this much of the more formal pattern of business meetings of larger organizations because it is necessary to know what is expected of a committee, in order for it to know how to fulfill its commitment. This is one of two major points of linkage between the small group process and the rules of procedure appropriate to the management of larger meetings. The other point at which they meet and overlap occurs when a large meeting recognizes the need to relax its usual rules in order to accomplish a specific purpose, and declares that it will, until that purpose has been achieved, behave as if it were a committee. Traditionally, the parliamentary rule books have provided for this maneuver through the motion "to resolve into a committee of the whole." Some few of the more recent codes substitute the motion "to consider informally." An explanation of these motions will serve to point up the differences between committee procedures and legislative or business meetings.

Committee of the Whole

The "committee of the whole" is composed of everyone attending the business meeting that adopts the motion creating it. The effect of the motion is to relax the operating rules so that a particular subject can be considered more informally. The motion can be adopted ("is in order") whenever a main motion is under discussion and there is the need or desire to discuss that motion without being restricted by the usual rules. When the motion is adopted the entire organization is automatically converted into a committee, with power only to discuss and recommend action on the main motion. At this point, just as he would for any committee, the presiding officer appoints someone else to serve as chairman and yields the leadership of the meeting to that person, who calls the committee to order and performs the usual functions of a committee chairman in guiding the discussion on the topic toward a report to be acted upon by the members of the organization. When the topic has been sufficiently considered and the report composed the committee votes to "rise and report," the presiding officer resumes his post, the business meeting is again in session and the formal rules are again in force.

The major effect of changing from formal rules to committee rules is that proposals may be made and discussed without presenting them as motions. By this means it is possible to develop or evolve a motion without using the process of amendment. "Straw votes" to test the sentiments of the members can be taken without binding the organization to a course of action. Consensus can be developed so that the motion that is finally presented through the report of the committee of the whole is essentially certain of adoption.

In practice, all but the largest, most formal organizations find this procedure unnecessarily cumbersome. Changing chairmen, adopting a report which has just been approved by the same body of people seemingly pretending they were somebody else, recessing and reconvening — all seem to tax the patience and imagination of organization members. For this reason authors of parliamentary codes for the present-day semi-business, semi-social organizations have provided a similar but less complex way to achieve the same relaxation of the rules. This is the motion for "informal consideration."

Informal Consideration

"Informal consideration" is appropriate under the same circumstances that generate the demand for the committee of the whole. The net effect is the same. The difference between the two motions is in the degree of ease with which that effect is accomplished. When a member says "I move informal consideration of . . ." and that motion is seconded and adopted by a simple majority of those voting, the chairman simply states that "the floor is now open for informal discussion on the motion to. . . ." He retains his chairmanship. The meeting is not recessed. There is no need to call the committee to order. Nor is there need to develop a report which must be acted upon twice by everyone present. Proposals can be offered, subjected to test votes, modified, dismissed (without the need to "withdraw"), and a motion can be developed that has a good chance of being adopted. When someone believes that he can offer such a motion, he has only to say "Mr. Chairman, I move that . . ." At that moment — without further ado — the meeting is restored to formal rules, and informal consideration is automatically shut off. The motion is then acted upon in the usual manner, and the meeting proceeds normally.

PURPOSE DETERMINES FORMALITY

Much has been said here about the differences between the formality of rules governing committee consideration and the rules governing action in the larger, parent organizations. Some of these differences lie in the different stages of problem-solving with which the two kinds of organizations are concerned. The committee, being assigned a problem to investigate, is in no position to bring its business to the floor through a motion proposing action. It must be concerned with the early stages of problem analysis in order to develop a basis from which to derive a proposal. The committee to which a motion is referred is likewise in that position. Though the action or policy proposition is before them, their task is to investigate the circumstances that led to the proposal and to recommend on the basis of their investigation the adoption, amendment, substitution, or rejection of the proposition. It makes sense, therefore, that the committee should consider a topic rather than a motion at the start, and, through a process of developing areas of agreement, should proceed in the direction of the action or policy proposal that will be the major factor of its report. After there has been some indication of preference among possible alternatives, the member or the chairman who feels that he senses this preference should attempt to word the motion which he believes can be generally accepted as the best thinking of the group. This minimizes the need for amendment. The proposed motion can, in committee, be amended simply by offering a suggestion that would change the wording, and securing agreement that the alternative suggestion is preferred. The greater the amount of agreement among committee members, the less need there is for formality, even at the final stages of committee action. It should, however, be absolutely clear to each member of the committee just what he is agreeing to as a part of the report.

Every member of the committee has his own personal right and duty to be correctly represented in the committee report. His name is usually appended to the report. As it is put there it is reasonable for the other members of the committee, as well as members of the parent organization, to assume that he knows and agrees with what is said in the report. The committee member, then, should take pains to know what the report contains and to be prepared to support any action proposed in the report. If, on the other hand, he does not feel that he can support what the majority of the committee has agreed upon, he ought to make his position clear through a minority report in collaboration with any others who share his views, or as an individual stating his own position.

SUMMARY

Committees that manage their meetings according to the principles of good conversational etiquette, working toward their ultimate goal of a useful report developed through problem-solving analysis, are using the necessary parliamentary considerations of respect for individual rights. As agreement is secured on intermediate goals, each committee progresses toward the recommendations of the information report that the parent organization requires. When an entire organization wants to function with the informal committee procedures because it is early in the stages of investigating a problem, it can do so most readily by adopting a motion for "informal consideration" of the problem.

Chapter 6

PARLIAMENTARY PRACTICE IN BUSINESS MEETINGS

Parliamentary practice in large business meetings (groups of forty or fifty or more) is nothing more or less than good etiquette adapted to the number of people involved. The same underlying tenets of good behavior described for committees control actions in the larger business meeting: each individual member's rights are sustained, the majority rules, and the goal is to get the most accomplished in the least time.

While it is true that there are these fundamental similarities, the differences between committees and meetings seem substantial. Many people who get along well in committees have great difficulty in participating effectively and comfortably in the more formal business meetings, where there always seems to be some "rule" known only to a few that confuses all the others. The confusion is generated largely by the fact that as people get concerned about the details of rules, they lose sight of their primary goal. Where the concern is to achieve results rather than to "obey the rules," things get done — and usually it is found that the rules were followed. This is because the rules have been derived from generations of observation of that procedure which best achieved results.

DECISIONS DEMAND FORMALITY

The major difference between committee and business meetings lies in the different tasks that confront each. As explained in the preceding chapter, the task of the committee — no matter whether it is to develop a plan of action in a recognized problem area or to evaluate a solution already proposed and make recommendations to the parent organization — is investigative in nature. The committee meeting demands more creative and imaginative thinking than does the business meeting. It demands more adaptation of ideas and less commitment to the defense of a previously determined position. Small committee size is determined by the knowledge that this kind of thinking is best carried on when people are least bound by rules. It has often been observed that when large groups become concerned with details they become very inefficient. Large groups must operate with too many rules to permit efficient creative or adaptive thinking.

It is true that adaptive and creative thinking thrive under minimum rule conditions. It is equally true that when decisions are necessary and when opposing arguments must be advanced to help determine those decisions, there is a need for rules to insure fair treatment and protection of everyone's rights and interests. Equally important is the democratic principle of permitting as many members of an organization as possible to participate in making the final decision. This, of course, means that the ideal meeting includes as many members as can be present when the time comes to vote. Thus both the demands for fair debate and the desire for maximum numbers point to the need for formal procedure in business meetings.

BASIS OF FORMALITY

The single fundamental difference between rules governing committee meetings and those governing business meetings derives from the provision that *the only way* to bring anything before a formal business meeting is to propose a motion ("Mr. Chairman, I move that . . ."). All of the rules of parliamentary procedure derive from and depend on the motion. Much or all of the confusion in the semi-formal, semi-social meetings in which we participate starts with an attempt to apply a rule when there is no motion, or to create a motion so that rules can apply in a situation that has been operating under the general principles of conversational etiquette. There are ways to make easy transitions between degrees of formality so that everyone knows what is happening and so that no rights are jeopardized and no feelings are hurt. One way is explained in the preceding chapter as the "Committee of the Whole"; another, also cited, is the motion for "Informal Consideration."

In the committee meeting a general idea (one which is at the investigation ("Let's talk about . . .") stage rather than at the solution-proposal ("I move that . . .") stage can be opened to discussion because it is possible for every member of the group to speak about the idea and help to give it shape without taking an inordinate amount of time. In this way, after it has been talked about for a while, a motion can be developed that will be accepted by at least a majority of the committee. In so doing almost everyone can exercise his right to speak and to be heard. On the other hand, when fifty or one hundred or a thousand people are members of the meeting, it is not practical to permit everyone to speak, or even to permit a few to speak as long as they wish without some limit on time. If anyone's right to speak and to be heard is to be limited it is only fair that everyone's right to speak should be limited equally. These are the conditions which are assured when every item of business is brought to the floor in the form of a motion.

A motion is a statement proposing that the group take an action or express a viewpoint. It is offered for discussion by the members so that they can determine whether they want to accept or reject the proposal. This is what gives form and purpose to the meeting. The rules determine how to proceed efficiently in considering the proposal and how it should be disposed. As organizations change in their nature and purpose, procedural rules are modified to conform to the new situations just as new practices appear in the patterns of acceptable social behavior. As new situations become common and as there is new understanding of how people work together, organizations adopt their own individual modifications of traditional rules. If these successfully serve their function they are adopted into new standard codes of procedure.

Once an organization has accepted the idea that all business must be brought up in the form of a motion (by introducing it with the words "I move that . . ."), the chairman or leader is granted a very clear way to keep his meeting moving along: until there is a motion, no one may speak. And when the motion is properly before the group, anything that is said *must* be related to that motion. Only after a motion has been properly disposed of may a member propose that the group talk about a different topic. When thought of in this way, it becomes clear that this basic rule is in essence the rule of conversational good behavior that deems it rude to interrupt the discussion of one topic by turning to another before the participants in the first discussion are finished.

CHAIRMAN'S FORMAL FUNCTION

Just as the host has the primary responsibility to guide social conversation, the chairman has the responsibility of making sure that parliamentary rules are fairly enforced, so that each member's rights are maintained. However, because he has more people to control, the chairman is expected to behave differently from the host. In comparison, the host might be likened to the schoolboy patrol whose job it is to keep the children from walking across the street when a car is approaching. He is stationed at those corners where there is not much traffic. He is not expected to stop the cars, but to caution the children who might get careless. On that same corner, on Saturday afternoons in the fall, there might be extremely heavy automobile traffic as cars go to and from a football game. Under these circumstances we do not rely on the schoolboy patrol, but we station an adult uniformed policeman who has been granted authority by law to direct traffic. Each motorist must wait for the policeman's signal. If he does not, he may break a law and he may damage someone's property, thereby infringing on that person's rights. The traffic policeman is expected to enforce the laws equally, not letting some drivers proceed while ignoring others altogether. He himself does not get involved in the traffic flow. The chairman, likewise, is expected to direct the discussion without any show of preference for one person or one idea over another. He is not expected to get involved in the substance of the discussion by offering his views as a part of the traffic of ideas. When a driver wants to turn in front of another car, he signals the policeman who controls all traffic, not just the other driver. It is the policeman who decides who will move first — whose rights will be honored first — in accordance with the best interests of equality among everyone. Thus it is that each person desiring to speak — to move in the stream of traffic of ideas — signals his desire to the chairman, and the chairman recognizes the member for the purpose that he indicated. If that purpose is not consistent with the law, the chairman will withhold or withdraw his approval. All of the communication in the formal parliamentary meeting is directed to and through the chairman, who retains control of the movement of the traffic of ideas and lets each member participate in turn according to the impartial procedure provided by parliamentary law.

Having established the principle that all business must be brought before a meeting in the form of a motion, the traditions of parliamentary procedure have provided a number of different ways in which such business can be handled. Fundamental to all business transactions is the practice of providing opportunity to explore and understand the meaning of each motion. This exploration and understanding, achieved through discussion and debate, gives the members the time to make up their minds whether to accept or reject the motion — whether to vote "aye" or "nay." The only exceptions to this general practice are those motions which are, by their nature, self-explanatory or which cannot be altered without defeating the intent of the motion itself. The motion to close debate (previous question), for instance, is not debatable because there is no doubt about its intent, and any alteration through amendment would defeat the intent of the motion. In this and similar cases the motion proceeds immediately from proposal to a vote.

All action that is to be binding upon the organization must be taken on the basis of a vote that determines the will of the majority of members. Almost all of the business that an organization transacts will be subject to a simple majority vote. This means that the side that receives more than half of the votes cast wins; in case of tie votes, the motion is defeated. There are some special circumstances that dictate different voting strengths needed for adoption, and these will be treated later.

There are some who hold that voting encourages contention and divides the members of the organization against each other. These advocates suggest that consensus must be achieved (i.e. everyone must agree) in order to be "democratic." This contention only demonstrates a misunderstanding of the concept of "democracy," which means that every member of the society has equal status with the other. Only through the principle of majority rule can this kind of democratic equality be achieved; the principle of consensus absolutely denies democracy.

EQUALITY OF VOTE

When seeking consensus, each member has a tyrannical rule over every other. When *every* member of an organization *must* agree in order to adopt a motion, any single member can frustrate the will of every other member simply by withholding his consent. This gives a minority of one complete control over a majority comprised of all members except that one. On the other hand, when only a majority vote is needed for action, each person has the same potential effect on the outcome as does every other person. No one person really "casts the deciding vote" because without the others who voted with him, he could be only a minority of one.

CONSENSUS

This is not said to deplore the efforts of any group which achieves consensus. There is absolutely no harm — and much good — when every member of an organization agrees with every other member. Where consensus is possible, every reasonable means should be used to encourage it. There are numbers of instances in meetings where routine matters need the approval of the members and where no reasonable opposition can be expected. At such times the chairman should encourage consensus through the use of the "common consent" vote ("Unless there is objection, we shall accept the report of the committee. /Pause/ No objection appearing, we shall declare the report accepted."). On the other hand, where differences of opinion may be expected to exist, the equality of member rights and the democracy shown through the principle of majority rule is the direct parallel of the equality experienced in social conversion, where each participant has the opportunity to voice his views but may be outnumbered by the majority of others.

MAJORITY RULE — MINORITY RIGHTS

As has been said earlier, the principle of majority rule is integrally tied to the principle of minority rights, and vice versa. Just as the majority cannot establish special limits on the rights of minorities, so the minority is pledged to accept the action taken by a majority and to help the organization to implement whatever decisions are made. Indeed, this is the principle which Thomas Jefferson cited as the fundamental of the entire system of parliamentary law. Jefferson, author of the rules under which the United States Congress operates, stated that rejection of the idea that the minority must join in implementation of decisions made by majority action amounted to a rejection of the entire basis for democratic government. It would make a confederation out of a federal union and an anarchy out of a representative government. Certainly it has become an established practice in both state and federal government that the two major political parties contend strongly for control of the executive and the legislative branches of the government until elections are held; after the votes are counted the majority determines the trend of policy and the minority supports the acts of the government even though they may have opposed those acts before the election. Only on very rare occasions will a citizen move from one state to another or move out of the country following an election because he feels that he cannot remain a member of that society. Most of us continue to remain members of the society in which we exercise our right to vote, and we obey the laws that are passed because after a time we will have another chance to create a different majority and perhaps to modify those laws. It is much the same with our membership in voluntary societies. Though it demands far less to resign from an organization than it does to move to another nation, members seldom even register this sort of protest when they find themselves in a minority. After slight or no protest, almost all members will "close ranks" and do their share in implementing decisions made in the name of the organization.

PARLIAMENTARY COMMON LAW

In addition to the principles of equality of vote and of majority rule, the third important consideration respecting the importance of voting in business meetings is that the record of the vote has become a part of the common laws of contract enforceable in civil courts.

Parliamentary procedure has grown in the same society and through the same slow historical development as the common law. When men grouped together to enter into contracts the same basic laws came to obtain as applied to individuals: anyone acting in the name of a group or organization could act only as the records of that organization would show that the majority directed. him to act; conversely, when he was instructed by the vote of the organization to sign a contract in the name of the organization, the organization itself was liable for executing the provisions of the contract. Legal partnerships provide that all persons who are partners are bound by contracts; corporation laws establish a "person" which acts in accord with the majority vote of those people who constitute its board of directors. In each case, civil law provides that a vote must be taken and made a part of the written records of the organization in order for a contract to be binding, and that once action is taken to implement the vote, the organization is bound by the terms of the contract. In this way it becomes impossible for an individual or minority group to avoid the commitment to organizational policy that their membership entails. Thus, if the junior class at the high school votes to hire "The Melodiers" dance band for the prom and this vote is recorded in the minutes, the following will be true:

1. The president of the class will be obliged to execute in the name of the class a contract with (and only with) "The Melodiers" for the prom. (If the president contracts with any other dance band he, not the class, is obligated to fulfill the contract).
2. If the president does execute a proper contract, the junior class, not the president, is obligated to fulfill the contract.
3. The dance band is obligated to play as specified in the contract with the junior class, not as directed by the president.

While it is true that some of the circumstances suggested here are seldom if ever going to happen, they do point out the significance of votes taken on business proposed for action in a business meeting. Each member thus has an obligation both to himself and to the organization to know the significance of every vote; to know what the results will be if he votes "yes" or "no." An ill-considered vote can lead to commitments that are binding and might be devastating to the organization. At the same time, commitment to membership in an organization and participation in its meetings demands a commitment to become informed and to cast well-considered votes that enable the organization to develop and execute important actions.

SPECIAL SITUATIONS DEMANDING
SPECIAL VOTING PROVISIONS

It was mentioned earlier that in certain specific circumstances decisions should be made on some basis other than a simple majority of those voting. All of these situations can be categorized as actions that will, in some way, limit the rights of some members. Where fundamental member rights are to be limited a larger proportion of the members must favor adoption of the action.

Unless it is otherwise specified in the rules of the particular organization, a "majority vote" means a simple majority of those casting votes on the motion. An organization of any size can, then, be committed by as little as a single vote if only one of the members cast his vote on a particular measure. Or if two members voted in favor of a motion and one voted against, the majority of two would suffice to commit the organization. This fact makes it obvious that while each member has the right not to vote on any given issue, it is in his best interests and the interests of the organization that he casts his vote. Only by voting does a member protect himself and his organization from being ruled by a minority. Any votes cast simply as "present" or "no vote" do not count as definitive votes in such cases. Departures from this common parliamentary law practice must have been specified prior to the vote if they are to supersede this interpretation.

The most frequent example of a situation in which member rights are limited is the motion to "close debate," or to "vote immediately." Generally, each member has an unlimited right to discuss and debate a motion, unless the general rules of the organization provide for some time limit, as is true of very large organizations. Even then, as the members adopt their rules they collectively agree to limit equally the right or freedom of everyone. But when a motion has been brought before an organization that does not normally restrict debate, any proposal to limit debate to a specified length of time or to stop debate before everyone who so wishes has had his chance to speak, represents an unusual limitation. If fifty-one of a hundred members want to stop the debate and vote immediately, this means that forty-nine, whose right to debate further would be limited by this action, will be silenced. At that point, if any one of the majority changed his vote, a motion to vote immediately would fail. This is a critical point, then. Traditionally, parliamentary practice has been to require a more dominant majority (usually two-thirds) to adopt such a motion limiting member rights. With a majority of this size, twice as many members want to stop debate and proceed to vote as want to discuss it further.

Some organizations require that motions demanding expenditure of funds be adopted by more than the usual simple majority. One such provision would be that instead of requiring a majority of those voting, a majority vote of *all* those present might be necessary, or even a majority of the entire membership. Under these circumstances staying away from the meeting, or declining to vote, has the same effect as the "no" vote.

Amendments to the fundamental documents of an organization almost always require more than a simple majority vote. Most even require formal written notice to the members *before* the meeting. These actions fall within the category of motions that might limit member rights. First, such an amendment would change some aspect of the basic structure of the organization, and each member already has given approval to the existing structure, so he should get a chance to decide whether he wants it changed or not. This suggests the need for prior notification enabling the member to make a special effort to attend the meeting and cast his vote. Often the standing rules and/or the by-laws can be amended through either of two ways: 1. prior notification plus a substantial majority (often 2/3), or, 2. an even higher majority (3/4 or 5/6) if permitted without prior notification. Almost without exception, amendments to the constitution of an organization demand prior notification and a substantial majority (2/3 or more) vote for adoption. Where both constitution and by-laws exist, the difficulty of amendment should be different and distinct between the two.

SUMMARY

Parliamentary practice in business meetings differs from that of committee meetings because the purpose of the business meeting is to arrive at a decision through discussion and debate, while the purpose of the committee meeting is to arrive at a proposal through investigation of a problem and its possible solutions. The business meeting begins with the product of the committee meeting — a proposal, stated as a motion — and operates under rules designed to provide for orderly and equitable consideration of that motion. The presiding officer controls the proceedings by enforcing the rules impartially, assuring full and fair discussion and protection of the rights of each member. Motions are adopted by a majority vote, which assures equality of the importance of each vote and conforms with the decisions of common law courts. Motions that have the effect of limiting the rights of any member through a change in usual procedure or a modification in the fundamental organization of a group require a proportionately larger majority of votes for adoption than do the usual items of business.

Chapter 7

EVERYDAY PARLIAMENTARY MOTIONS

"MR. CHAIRMAN, I MOVE. . . ."

This is the only way to introduce a motion in a parliamentary meeting! Any other preface to a motion is as out of place as a baseball glove on a basketball court. One does not need any more; one cannot do the job with any less; and any variations on this form only serve to obscure the intent of what one is saying. If you "suggest" that a party be planned, or that discussion be stopped, your chairman will not know whether you mean to offer a motion or not. He will have to ask you to "put that in the form of a motion." By this he means that you should say, "Mr. Chairman (or you may omit this because you have already been recognized and given the floor for the purpose of making the motion), I MOVE. . . ." The next word is almost inevitably either "that" or "to," followed by the rest of the sentence. The rest of the sentence will determine what sort of motion is being proposed.

The motion that proposes that the organization take some sort of action — such as sponsor a dance, send a letter to the Congressman, collect dues, buy a book — is called the *main* or *substantive motion*. Likewise, the motion that proposes that the organization express a specific viewpoint — such as to recommend a change in foreign policy, to request a review of textbook costs, or to go on record as favoring a tax reduction — is a main or substantive motion in the form of a recommendation, a petition, or a resolution. This form is appropriate when the organization lacks the power to act directly, but wants to let those who have that power know their collective sentiments.

The main motion is the basis for all procedural rules. Without the main motion no business is brought before the meeting. By the same token, when a main motion is properly brought up for consideration it constitutes the only focus of attention until it is disposed of. No other main motion can be considered until some action has been recorded clearly indicating the decision of the members with respect to the pending motion. This decision may be one of three kinds: a simple decision to accept or reject; a decision to modify (amend) followed by acceptance or rejection; or decision to postpone final action in one of several ways.

MAIN MOTION MANAGEMENT

It is clear, then, that because our concern is effective meeting management it is also effective main motion management. When we are concerned with what we want to accomplish, rather than trying to remember rules, we can describe what might happen to a motion and thus understand the rules which govern how a main motion should be handled in a meeting. In so doing we shall be describing the manner in which about 90 per cent of the business is managed in 98 per cent of the meetings which we shall attend.

First and foremost, the main motion must be made in proper form. A member must seek and receive recognition from the chairman. This gives the member the floor so that he, and only he, is the one to whom everyone should be listening. The member should state his proposal clearly and briefly. The chairman should then provide an opportunity for someone else in the organization to indicate that he, too, is willing to devote some of the meeting time to a discussion of the proposal by seconding the motion. This may be done with or without formal recognition by the chairman, depending on the group's customary degree of formality. In most instances a motion will receive a "second" almost automatically. But where there is no second immediately forthcoming, the chairman should ask for one as a warning that if no one but the person who offered the motion believes that it is worth considering, the organization will not take time to discuss it. If no second is offered, the motion dies. If it does receive a second, the chairman then restates the motion and asks the members to discuss the motion and to start to determine how they want to act on it.

The pattern for offering a main motion is simple but basic to the conduct of the meeting. The more often the correct form is practiced, the more familiar and comfortable the members of the organization will become with it and the easier it will be to conduct a meeting efficiently and correctly. The dialogue should be as follows:

ENGLEHART: Mr. Chairman. (In relatively informal meetings, the member may simply raise his hand, or rise without speaking.)

CHAIRMAN: Mr. Englehart. (Or he may use the first name, if the group is relatively small and is well acquainted.)

ENGLEHART: I move that the Zook Club contribute $10.00 from its treasury to the United Fund.

CHAIRMAN: Is there a second to the motion? (Often another member will simply say "second" without waiting for the chairman to ask, or to recognize him.)

CHAIRMAN (continuing, after the second has been heard): It has been moved and seconded that the Zook Club contribute $10.00 from its treasury to the United Fund. The floor is now open for discussion on the motion. (The question "Is there any discussion?" is often used, but this might suggest that there is doubt that discussion will be forthcoming, and this tends to squelch the member who isn't quite sure that his comments or questions are worth the time they might take.)

The example above is a motion submitted in good form. It is both clear and brief. If the member has said "I move that we contribute $10.00 to charity," it would have raised several questions. The proposal might intend that each individual member contribute $10.00 personally or that a special collection be taken to make up the amount. Likewise, "charity" is a generic term which leads to differing interpretations. With a motion such as this, it is doubly important that the chairman clarify the motion as he restates it to put it before the members for discussion. He does this by modifying the original wording to specify the intent of the member who offers the proposal. He should propose a wording for the motion that will state the idea more clearly and seek agreement from the proposer.

A second category of motions needing clarification is demonstrated by the member who thinks aloud as he is recognized, saying, "I believe that we have enough in our treasury to justify some support by our club for the United Fund Drive, so I say we ought to give $10.00. Mr. Chairman, I move that." When it appears here, in print, following an example of a properly phrased motion, this motion is obviously in bad form, but it occurs with great regularity in meetings of all types. Poorly phrased motions place the responsibility on the chairman to create a proper motion from the member's ideas both for the benefit of the members who are to discuss it and for the secretary whose job it is to record the action. When the chairman is careful that motions are put into proper form, he sets an example that the members will tend to follow.

Once the motion is properly stated by the chairman, the normal pattern is to hear some discussion — a line of reasoning that supports the adoption of the proposal, questions seeking some detailed information about how the plan will work, who will be responsible, or what would happen if the motion is defeated — and finally to bring the motion to a vote. More often than not, a motion offered is a motion adopted. A constructive proposal is more appealing than the alternative of doing nothing. But there are often good reasons for changing the initial motion before committing the organization to action, and there are times when it is inadvisable or even impossible to take final action at the time a motion is offered. These facts give rise to one category of secondary motions: the subsidiary motions, which have meaning only as they apply to a main motion. Generally, because there are three ways in which it is possible to take action other than immediate adoption or rejection, there are three categories of subsidiary motions: motions to alter the substance of the main motion, motions to delay or defer final action, and motions to limit debate on the motion in some way.

AMENDING

If discussion of Mr. Englehart's motion to contribute $10.00 from the Zook Club treasury to the United Fund showed that some members thought that the club could afford more generous support of this particular agency, these members would have two possible courses of action: they could either work to defeat this motion and immediately propose a new motion specifying a higher amount, or they could move to amend (propose to change the wording of) the motion already before them. The latter is the more efficient way to proceed, because it more clearly identifies the fact that they support the idea, but differ on a single specific aspect of the proposal.

A main motion may be amended by deletion, by addition, or by substitution (a combination of the other two). In this instance, the proper motion would be stated as follows:

CHAIRMAN: Mr. Bush.

BUSH: I move to amend the motion to delete (or strike) the word "ten" and substitute the word "twenty."

MEMBER: Second.

CHAIRMAN: It has been moved and seconded to amend the motion to substitute the word "twenty" for the word "ten," so that the motion would read "the Zook Club contributes $20.00 from its treasury to the United Fund." We are now ready for discussion on the amendment.

At this point the discussion must focus on the desirability of the $20.00 figure in comparison with the $10.00 sum originally proposed. The person who is opposed to any contribution at all should wait until a vote is taken on the amendment and discussion again is on the main motion (or the amended main motion, if the proposed change is favored by a majority of those voting). In terms of the old familiar rule that "there can be only one motion before the house at any one time," the amendment itself constitutes the single motion under discussion until it is acted upon.

Two limitations are usually placed on the motion to amend: (1) amendments must be germane to the main motion, and (2) there should be not more than one amendment to an amendment pending at any time. A third limitation is sometimes added: no amendment that simply reverses or negates the original motion shall be accepted.

"Germaneness" is not always an easy quality to agree upon. It means "related to," and there are those who contend that everything is related to something else, so there is nothing unrelated in the world. In a more limited sense, if an amendment were proposed to add the phrase "and that the club sponsor a Bingo game next Friday afternoon" to the original motion proposing a United Fund contribution, there would be a real question whether the Bingo game was related to the proposed contribution. In this case, the chairman would rule to recognize the amendment or not on the basis of his view of its relevance to the original main motion. If he rules the amendment out of order because it was not germane, the proponent would have the right to appeal from the decision of the chair to determine how many other members wanted to discuss it. If the decision of the chairman were upheld, the proposed amendment would be out of order at that time. If his decision were reversed, the amendment would be recognized as proper, and discussion and a vote would be the next item of business.

As any amendments are adopted, the wording of the original motion is altered to include the amendment, and discussion then focuses on the motion as changed. The final vote, after the motion is amended to suit the majority and after there has been adequate discussion so that the members have made up their minds how they want to vote, is taken on the main motion in its amended form. Thus, Mr. Englehart's original motion, following the adoption of the proposed amendment, would be put to a vote by the chairman:

> All of those who favor the motion that the Zook Club contribute $20.00 from its treasury to the United Fund please raise your hands. Those opposed to the motion raise your hands. The motion carries and the contribution will be made (or the motion is defeated).

DEFERRING FINAL ACTION

Despite the rule that when a main motion is brought before an organization it must be disposed of in one way or another before any other motion is in order, there are occasions when it is neither possible nor desirable to take final action at the time a motion is proposed. At these times it is necessary to take some action that will dispose of the pending motion for the moment, but will leave it open for action by the organization at a later time. Often this situation develops when a main motion is proposed in a meeting with a full agenda and one or more members seek to change it through the amending process, or when the issue is relatively unfamiliar to the members. As the discussion proceeds without notable progress toward consensus, it becomes apparent that unless the matter is disposed of in some way, the agenda will not be completed. At other times it is obvious that the members need some time to think about the proposal in order to avoid an ill-considered action.

Returning to Mr. Englehart's motion that his organization contribute $10.00 to the United Fund as an illustration, it is easy to see how this motion might tie up a meeting for a long time. There are all sorts of considerations which may be important to the vote. The budget may be relatively fixed, without provision for this contribution. If it is approved, something else might have to be curtailed. The question of precedent might be raised: if they make this contribution this year, are they binding themselves to continue to do so annually? Is this the best way to support community welfare, or are other ways better? Would other ways of securing the funds be preferable? These and other questions would have a bearing on the vote on this motion. Also, it might be difficult to oppose the adoption of such a motion because of the implication that the organization is not sympathetic to the purposes of the United Fund, no matter what the real bases were for defeating the motion.

The traditions of parliamentary procedure have assigned a specific order of precedence to those motions which defer final action. They are arranged so that there is a logical reason not to permit the lower precedence motions to be made while the higher ranking motion is pending, but that a vote on the higher ranking motion can and does make sense before taking action on any lower ranking motions which may have preceded it. The rank order of precedence is as follows:

1. The motion to lay on the table
2. The motion to postpone definitely
3. The motion to refer to a committee
4. (The motion to amend)
5. The motion to postpone indefinitely

Postponing Indefinitely

The motion to postpone indefinitely is designed to remove a main motion from the floor without defeating it, but without any commitment to entertain it further. This is the motion that is appropriate for a motion such as Mr. Englehart's, when the organization does not want to approve the contribution, but does not want to be on record as having opposed making a United Fund contribution. It is the only motion that should be used with the intent of avoiding positive action. It has received the lowest order of precedence because in most instances an organization should be prepared to take positive action either favoring or opposing a proposal. It is highly probable, then, that through one or another of the deferring motions a motion will be framed that will clarify the situation so that the matter can be settled more definitely.

For instance, if some members object to Mr. Englehart's motion on grounds that it may establish a precedent, and are therefore inclined to postpone action indefinitely, an amendment (discussed above, and not strictly a postponing motion) might be offered that would read "I move that the Zook Club contribute $10.00 from its treasury to the United Fund for this year only." The proposed amendment would resolve the question of establishing a precedent and focus the issue on the contribution, or on where it was to come from, which could then prompt some of the members to act decisively.

The motion to postpone has undergone a history that has led to differing practices in different organizations. One path has led to the practice of treating the motion to postpone indefinitely (without a time fixed for further consideration) as a separate and distinct motion from the motion to postpone to a certain time. The other path has treated these as two forms of the same motion. In both cases, the rules governing the motion are essentially the same; it is always debatable; the motion in its indefinite form is not amendable (the motion to postpone to a certain time has a higher rank of precedence, so it can be offered and acted upon just as if it were an amendment to the motion to postpone indefinitely), while the motion to postpone to a certain time can be amended with respect to the time specified; both require a simple majority for adoption. In order to make the two motions rank separately, the provision has been made that the motion to postpone to a certain time may *not* be amended to change its effect to that of the motion to postpone indefinitely, as would be the case if a member proposed: "Mr. Chairman, I move that we postpone consideration of the motion to invite Joe Josephson to speak at our February meeting until our meeting scheduled for March 19." Prohibition of obvious misuse of a motion is in the same tradition that provides that no amendment should be considered that would simply reverse or negate the effect of a motion. At the same time, it can reasonably be argued that the question of whether a motion should ever be considered again or not is simply one alternative among the range of alternative times at which it might be considered.

In sum, it seems less confusing to treat the motion to postpone consideration as one single, amendable motion, irrespective of the length of time specified. In those rare instances where a question of precedence might arise, the chairman should rule in favor of the course of action that makes the best sense in the situation, always subject to an appeal from his decision.

Referring to a Committee

Almost as frequently as someone might offer a proposal to amend, a member may seek recognition and say: "Mr. Chairman, I move to refer the motion before the house to a committee for study and a report at our next meeting."

Adoption of this motion would then place the main motion, together with any amendments and even the motion to postpone action indefinitely, in the hands of either a Standing Committee or a Special Committee (see Chapter V), and clear the floor for further business.

Note that the motion as stated above is more precise than many that are offered to place a matter in the hands of a committee at most of our meetings. This motion specified what the committee should do with the main motion (i.e., "study" it) and when they were to report. It is obvious from the way the motion is stated that it is not the intent of the proposer to use the motion to commit as a substitute for the motion to postpone action indefinitely. He is recognizing that more thought on the matter is needed, and that a smaller group could handle it better than the larger one at this stage of consideration. He is recognizing also that it is usually within the perogatives and responsibilities of the chairman to determine the composition of the committee — whether it should be a standing or a special committee, and if the latter, who and how many should be appointed. This is normally done at or soon after the close of the meeting which refers a matter to a committee.

Postponing Definitely (to a Certain Time)

When there is good reason to act upon a matter at a later time, it is proper to propose that action be delayed until that time. Perhaps the organization is falling behind a published agenda and wants to permit further discussion later in the same meeting or at the following meeting. (Unless there is a special reason, postponement beyond the next meeting is not usually permitted. Such a reason might be that the motion requires the completion of an event or program, the election or appointment of new officers, etc.) Or, again, the matter might be postponed until later in the same meeting because more (or fewer) members might be expected to be present. In such a case, the dialogue would be:

CHAIRMAN: Is there any further discussion of the motion?

MEMBER: Mr. Chairman, I move to postpone the motion before the house until nine o'clock.

CHAIRMAN (following a second): The motion has been made and seconded to postpone the motion before the house until nine o'clock. Is there any discussion of this motion? . . . (After discussion, or a pause to permit discussion.) All of those in favor of postponing the motion until nine o'clock raise your hands. Those opposed. The motion carries and the matter is postponed until nine o'clock. Is there any further business?

When this action has been taken, the main motion will be brought back before the house as soon after nine o'clock as the floor is cleared of pending business. It is the responsibility of the chairman (often assisted by the secretary or parliamentarian) to place the matter again before the members. It cannot be brought up before the appointed hour, nor can the members refuse to consider it when the time comes unless they reverse their earlier action by a two-thirds majority vote. When they specify a time in postponing the motion the members have, in effect, created a rule which binds them unless they suspend the rules. This action always takes a two-thirds majority because it can mean that the rights of those members who have been led to believe that the vote will not be before the hour, and will be taken soon after, are being jeopardized.

(See discussion of "POSTPONING INDEFINITELY," page 58.)

Laying on the Table

The most familiar form of the motion to delay action is, "Mr. Chairman, I move that we lay the matter on the table." This wording stems from the practice in legislative bodies, such as the early United States Congress, that dealt with written motions handed to the secretary, which he then picked up from his table and read aloud to the members. If a more pressing matter was to be brought before them, a Congressman had only to move to "table" what was then before them. If the motion to table was adopted, the secretary laid down the first document for consideration at some unspecified later time, picked up the more significant motion and read it, thereby bringing it up for consideration. It was proper, then, after the more urgent business was accomplished for the Congress to instruct the clerk to pick up the motion again. Adoption of the motion, "Mr. Chairman, I move that the motion to . . . be taken from the table," was the way to achieve that goal. The motion to table was not debatable because its purpose was to provide a quick way to determine whether or not the organization wanted to give a higher priority to some other business. A "no" vote simply said that the assembly wanted to proceed with its consideration of the pending motion, or that it did not feel that there was enough urgency to set the pending business aside.

Several factors in the history of the motion to lay on the table have worked to make it known as an effective way to kill a proposed action without the danger of negative effects from voting directly against it (i.e., to create the same effect as the motion to postpone indefinitely). First, there was the growing number of motions, bills, and resolutions that made it less possible to return to the discussion of a tabled action. This led, in some organizations, to the requirement of a two-thirds majority to take a motion from the table. This requirement is in the spirit of equality of opportunity, because it can well be argued that it is fairer to discuss a motion not previously under discussion than to renew discussion of a motion that has been put down as being of less importance than other considerations. In other organizations the rule developed that consideration of a bill, once tabled, could not be renewed in the same session. The United States Congress, having one session each year, follows this practice. Some state legislatures having a session only every two years follow this same pattern, so the tabling of a motion does, in these instances, amount to a postponement of at least two years. In most business or voluntary organizations, however, which meet at regular and frequent intervals, such as once each week or month, the motion to lay on the table if properly used is for the sole purpose of giving a higher priority to some urgent business, while leaving the possibility open for later action on the tabled motion. The advantage in the motion to table compared with the motion to postpone is that the motion to table is not debatable, so there is no possibility of becoming sidetracked on debate over when to resume consideration (take from the table) of the pending motion. The motion to table should be used only rarely; the usual delaying motion would be the motion to postpone.

LIMITING DEBATE

Closing Debate

Of the four possible ways to limit debate on a main motion, the one most frequently used is the motion to close debate immediately. This is traditionally referred to as "the motion for the previous question." Because of this awkward wording, it has, perhaps, been the cause of more mistaken intentions in voting than any other motion. Many times members feel that they are voting on the main motion or on an amendment under discussion (i.e., voting on the question itself instead of on the "motion for the previous question"), when they are really voting on whether or not to close debate so that they can then proceed to vote on the substantive motion.

The motion to close debate is appropriate when a main motion or an amendment, or any debatable motion, has been under consideration long enough for most members to decide how to vote, but at a point when some members still seek to participate in the debate. This motion is not appropriate immediately following the statement of a debatable motion and should not be recognized (should be declared "out of order" by the chairman) until there has been some debate. Otherwise it would serve as a gag on all debate and would be contrary to the basic tenets of parliamentary rules. Neither is it really appropriate after everyone has had his say, when no one seeks recognition to continue debate. At this point the motion to close debate is unnecessarily cumbersome. All one has to do then is remain silent when the chairman asks if there is further debate on the motion under discussion.

In a large number of organizations the practice of saying "question" when ready to vote has become common, in order to inform the chairman that at least some of the members are ready to vote. This has become known as the "call for the question," and can be used as informal social pressure on those contemplating further debate. The chairman may acknowledge that a member has said "question" by saying, "The question has been called for, is there any further discussion on the motion?" Any member who feels that he has a new point, or who cannot bear the burden of an undelivered speech, still may seek recognition and speak. Every member should, however, recognize that at least some feel that the debate has lasted long enough. He should re-evaluate what he has to say in this light. It might be that he only intended to reinforce what has already been said, merely saying that he agreed with previous speakers. In this case, he should yield to the pressures and remain silent. On the other hand, when a member feels that he has a new or important point that might influence the outcome of the vote, he has every right and obligation to seek recognition. In this way he will contribute to an informed vote on the proposal.

Because the motion to close debate limits the general right of all members to debate a motion fully and freely, it has been established that more than a bare majority should be necessary to adopt the motion. As with other motions to limit debate, at least twice as many must favor the motion as the number that oppose it (a two-thirds majority in favor of the motion is needed) in order to close debate. The two-thirds figure has been accepted as a fair compromise between the safeguard for the rights of the minority and the acceptance of the rule of the majority.

The motion to close debate and its informal counterpart, the "call for the question," apply only to the motion under debate at the moment. This means that when an amendment is under consideration as the motion to close debate is offered, it applies only to that amendment. If it is felt that the entire matter — main motion plus one or two pending amendments — has been accorded enough attention, it is permissible to "move to close debate on all pending motions." If a two-thirds majority favors this motion, then a vote on the amendments and the main motion (perhaps as amended) may be taken without any further discussion.

The same situation holds true when any motions to defer action are pending. A motion to close debate adopted when the motion to refer to a committee is under discussion applies only to the motion to refer to a committee. If debate is closed and the motion to commit is defeated, discussion is then in order on the main motion, or on any pending amendments. The motion "to close debate on all pending motions" would be necessary if all discussion on the entire matter were to be brought to a close.

Setting Limits on Debate

The three remaining ways of limiting debate are variations on the same theme of specifying limits on the time that may be devoted to a particular motion. Except in rather large organizations these are seldom used, largely because they are cumbersome or awkward to enforce. If time is the criterion, it must be accurately kept, in order to be fair, and this usually requires a stop-watch. Interruptions may occur, giving rise to feelings of unequitable treatment. Unless there is a parliamentarian, or someone specially designated to keep time, these are not very useful limiting motions.

Nevertheless, they are possible and are effective ways of managing main motions. The three forms are as follows:

MR. CHAIRMAN, I move that each member be permitted to speak only once, for a maximum of five minutes on the motion pending.

MR. CHAIRMAN, I move that debate on the motion pending be limited to twenty minutes.

MR. CHAIRMAN, I move that the vote on the motion pending be taken no later than 4:00 P. M. (Note: if the motion were to read "taken at 4:00 P. M." it cannot be taken either before or after that time without suspending a rule.)

The form that specifies individual limits is the most difficult to enforce, but is more equitable. The motion specifying total elapsed time is easily convertible to the form proposing an hour at which debate must stop.

In each case, debate is permitted on the motion to limit, but is restricted, as is the possibility of amendment, to the amount of time specified. Because they limit member rights, each form requires a two-thirds majority vote to be adopted.

RECESS AND ADJOURNMENT

Recessing

There are times when the greater progress can be made by declaring that no progress is expected. When a meeting has reached the point where members are tired, perhaps hungry and contentious, it is wise to recess for a time, so that the members can return more relaxed. Recognition that physical comfort affects the workings of the mind is usually provided in the agenda of organizations that meet infrequently, but for long sessions. A two or three-day meeting is scheduled to provide for meals and usually for morning and afternoon rest periods. When breaks are not provided, or when the business itself suggests that the recess come earlier or later than the agenda proposes, the proper motion is:

MEMBER (after recognition): Mr. Chairman, I move that we recess for (fifteen) minutes.

CHAIRMAN (after a second is heard): The motion is to recess for (fifteen) minutes. Those who favor the motion please raise your hands. Those opposed. The motion is carried. We shall recess for (fifteen) minutes, until _____ o'clock.

The motion to recess is equally useful in shorter, more frequent meetings, where it almost always has a more strategic importance. One such situation occurs when discussion is proceeding on a main motion and it becomes apparent that no one in the meeting has the specific information necessary to the decision. If the debate can profitably proceed while one member goes off to seek the missing information, no recess is necessary. If there is no point to continuing until the information is available, the members will return to their work more agreeably if they enjoy a brief recess.

When debate has proceeded to the point where there seems to be a stalemate, where tempers are short, or where a "bandwagon" seems to be developing and a cooling off period is advisable before taking a vote on a substantive motion, the recess is equally useful. This gives a chance for some person-to-person exchange of ideas, which is not possible in a formal meeting and which often will reduce tensions and make the members more satisfied with the final results of a vote.

The motion to recess is privileged because it can be entertained while another motion is on the floor. It does not qualify as an emergency measure that can interrupt another speaker, because no member's rights are really being jeopardized if the motion is delayed for several minutes. Apart from permitting a brief statement setting forth reasons for a recess, the motion is not debatable when another motion is pending. If debate were possible, the motion could be used to distract from a main motion and would tend to confuse rather than facilitate accomplishment of the business at hand. Once defeated, the motion can be offered again at any time after some reasonable progress has been achieved.

If a recess is proposed when no other business is before the house, it is treated just as any main motion, and is debatable and amendable with respect to the length of time specified.

Adjourning

When the proposed agenda for a meeting has been accomplished, the only item which remains to complete the formal structure at a meeting is adjournment. At this time the chairman is in a position to say, "If there is no other business to come before us, I shall declare the meeting adjourned. (PAUSE) The meeting is adjourned." The *pause* is absolutely necessary in this process to assure that the members have an opportunity to declare any last-minute proposals or announcements. If there are none, this amounts to giving common consent to the motion to adjourn. It should *not* be so used that either the chairman or the members develop the feeling that the chairman has the right or power to adjourn the meeting. This he cannot do, any more than he can simply announce that a substantive motion is adopted or rejected.

The more formal process, and the one that must be used if there is any feeling that the members are not quite ready to go home, is as follows:

MEMBER (after recognition): Mr. Chairman, I move that we adjourn.

CHAIRMAN (after hearing a second): It has been moved and seconded that we adjourn. All in favor raise your hands. Those opposed. The motion carries and we stand adjourned.

Except in those rare occasions when it is appropriate to specify a time and place for the next meeting, the motion to adjourn is not debatable, because there is nothing to be accomplished by debate. If the majority of the members wants to adjourn, there is little point in trying to hold them further.

No meeting is actually adjourned until the chairman announces the result of the vote on the motion to adjourn. The other duties and responsibilities of the chairman may make it necessary for him to delay that announcement until he is assured that all important items of business and all announcements have been made. For that reason it is not only polite, but important to the completion of the meeting that each member remain in his seat until the chairman declares the meeting adjourned. Time will be lost if some members start to depart and must be called back. When the motion to adjourn comes to the floor after all regular business is completed, it is rather easy to make sure that everything is taken care of. When adjournment is moved while a substantive motion is under consideration, final announcements are more often neglected.

Adjournment while a substantive main motion, or one of the motions designed to defer action, is under consideration is sometimes necessary or advisable. If regular adjournment time has past and there is a real possibility of hasty and ill-considered action, it is often better to postpone final action than to take hasty or ill-considered action. When the majority does decide to adjourn before acting on a motion, that motion may be considered following the regular routine of opening the meeting. Essentially, then, the organization may pick up where they stopped at the previous meeting when the chairman announces that the floor is open for unfinished business.

SUMMARY

Motions are the basis of the formal parliamentary meeting. All procedural rules have developed as organizations have sought to consider motions (proposals) and to act upon them efficiently, abiding by the expressed will of the majority, and respecting the rights of each member.

The basic pattern of consideration for motions is: the statement of the proposal (the main or substantive motion) and discussion and debate of the proposal, including modification or amendment, leading to decision (acceptance or rejection by vote of the members). On occasion, it is impossible or undesirable to make a final decision on a motion, leading to the consideration of one or more of the ways of deferring action through postponement (indefinitely, or to a certain time), referring to a committee, or laying on the table. Provision is also made for avoiding unduly prolonged debate when a two-thirds majority favors limiting individual participation or total time for debate, or favors closing debate to vote immediately.

Knowledge of these fundamental motions governing the consideration of main motions will equip the participant in a formal meeting with the understanding and information necessary to act effectively in almost all (over 90 per cent) of every meeting. Other motions less frequently used, which may or may not grow out of the subject matter of discussion, will be explained in the following chapter.

Chapter 8

OTHER USEFUL MOTIONS

A second group of incidental motions is concerned with the rights of members. At any time when people are trying to work together for a common goal it is possible that the rights and privileges of any individual member may suffer at the hands of others. At the same time, it is possible that a single member, in a zealous effort to protect his individual rights, may transgress the rights of a number of other members. If parliamentary rules are to function, they must provide for some counterbalance, so that while the majority does prevail, the minority can be protected from a free-wheeling majority.

Because any situation that jeopardizes the rights of a member should be ended, motions seeking to clarify or support those rights need to be considered without delay. For that reason these motions can be offered while another person has the floor. In order that the chairman know that the member seeking recognition while a speaker is still talking does wish to propose a motion for immediate decision, the member must state the purpose for which he seeks recognition. When the chairman hears that purpose, he interrupts the speaker to find out specifically what it is that the other member has on his mind. One such situation occurs when a member has a question about the motion under consideration or about how to proceed properly.

REQUESTS FOR INFORMATION

If a meeting is to be successful, it is important that each member be kept informed of the status of the business and where the meeting might be heading. When a member is in doubt about the intent or effect of a motion, he should be able to ask a question either of a specific person or of the members in general, and he should be able to expect an answer. If he wishes to know how to accomplish something properly — what motion to propose, or what the effect of his vote will be — he must be able to raise a question and receive an answer. The rules do provide that a member may raise such a question. Because it would be awkward to put an inquiry in the usual form of a motion, the rules in this case provide for a slightly different way of addressing the chairman.

Request for Information

While the Zook Club is considering Mr. Englehart's motion, this dialogue might take place:

ENGLEHART: I have proposed this motion because I believe that we have adequate funds in our treasury to support our usual activities, and, at the same time . . .

MEMBER (interrupting): I rise for information, Mr. Chairman.

CHAIRMAN: What is your question?

MEMBER: I would like to know how much is now in our treasury, and how much of this is already committed to other activities.

CHAIRMAN: Can you (or "can the speaker") answer the question specifically at this time?

ENGLEHART: Not right down to dollars and cents.

CHAIRMAN: We can ask for a review of this information from the treasurer after you have concluded.

If the member had not identified his purpose as one that can legitimately interrupt a speaker, the chairman must rule him out of order and permit Englehart to continue. Once the purpose is established, there is a good deal of latitude in handling the question. Because the chairman is in control of the situation, he determines what actually does happen. If the member wants his answer from the speaker, he would proceed as follows:

MEMBER (interrupting): I rise for information, Mr. Chairman. I would like to ask Mr. Englehart a question.

CHAIRMAN: Will you yield to a question, Mr. Englehart?

ENGLEHART: Yes, I will yield. (Or "No, I would prefer not to yield at this point. Perhaps I will answer the question as I proceed; if not, I will respond to questions after I conclude." Or he may say, "No, I will not answer any questions.")

The third response should be used very rarely because it suggests that the speaker either fears that a question will do some damage to his cause (perhaps exposing a weakness in his knowledge or reasoning), or that he feels that the questioner may not be acting in good faith. Of course, either or both of these may be true, but it is usually better to assume that the question is an honest one and that the answer can be provided in such a way that it will help the business along. Note that it is seldom wise to offer a flat refusal to a question. The answer may be postponed, but a refusal constitutes both a denial of the tradition of full and open discussion and a poor tactic when seeking to persuade others to vote in favor of your position on a proposal.

When the question is one that the chairman can answer directly, he does so and then permits the speaker to resume. In the instance above, if the chairman felt that this information was needed immediately, he could call on the treasurer to answer before permitting Englehart to proceed. The chairman should exercise his discretion in keeping everyone concentrating on the issues at hand, rather than permitting personal feelings to become important.

It is important that everyone knows that questions are asked through the chairman, rather than directly by the questioner to the speaker. In the informal committee meeting it is possible to carry on direct dialogue between members without the intervention of the chairman, but in larger meetings the chairman must maintain control over the traffic of ideas, recognizing each speaker in turn.

Parliamentary Inquiry

When a member is in doubt about a motion or about the proper form to follow, his question takes the form of a parliamentary inquiry and is made by saying, "Mr. Chairman, I rise to a parliamentary inquiry." The chairman then replies, "State your inquiry." The member may then ask, "Is an amendment in order at this time?" or "I don't believe that we have enough information to act on this motion at this time; what is the best procedure for delaying action so that we can find out more about it?" To questions such as these the chairman provides an immediate answer, and the speaker then continues. If the chairman feels that the question does not have an immediate bearing on the progress of consideration of the main motion, he may wait before answering until the speaker has finished.

POINT OF ORDER

Closely related to the point of inquiry is the point of order. In this situation, as in the other, the member is essentially raising a question to be answered by the chairman. As the member says, "Mr. Chairman, I rise to a point of order," and the chairman replies, "State your point," the member may say, "I feel that Manfred is out of order because he is not talking about the motion before us." He is asking the chairman to decide who is right — the speaker or the member who raises the point of order. The chairman rules without putting the question to a vote of the membership. But just as in every other situation, it is as impossible for a chairman to force an organization to act against its will as it is for any other single member to enforce his individual will against a majority.

When the chairman announces his ruling on the point of order he will say "Your point is well taken," or "Your point is not well taken," and then suggest how the meeting is to proceed. If some rule of order is not being observed, the chairman should instruct the speaker to conform to the rules of the organization. If the chairman has mistakenly entertained a motion that should not be recognized, he should declare that motion out of order and explain to the members what then is the proper way to proceed. As he announces his decision and suggests what should be done, the chairman is, in essence, submitting his judgment for the common consent of the members. If they agree, their best course of action is to remain silent and let the meeting proceed as the chairman suggests. If, on the other hand, they do not agree, it is within the rights and duties of any member to put the chairman's decision to the test of a vote of the members.

APPEAL FROM THE DECISION OF THE CHAIR

The right of any member to appeal from the decision of the chair gives credence to the view that the chairman is, in fact, the servant of the organization over which he presides. He can make no ruling that is not supported, by action or by default, by a majority of the membership. Any member who feels that a chairman is acting in a peremptory or biased manner may appeal from that decision. It does no good for the member or for the organization to wait until the meeting is adjourned before complaining. This leads only to feelings of frustration and dissatisfaction. It shows that the objector either does not know that he has the right to appeal or that he feels that he is in a hopeless minority position, but wants to complain anyway. Where the members do know their rights no chairman can impose his decision in opposition to the desires of a majority.

A member institutes an appeal, interrupting a speaker if necessary, by saying, "Mr. Chairman, I appeal from the decision of the chair." Every decision of the chair is going to favor one side and rule against another. With the point of order, the chairman either rules in favor of the speaker or the person who raised the question of order. It can always be assumed, then, that at least one person may want to appeal the decision of the chairman. To make sure that he is not the only member disagreeing with the chairman (just as the rules provide that more than one member wants to consider any substantive motion), the appeal from the decision of the chair must be seconded. It should be the point of view of the seconder in this case, as in any situation requiring a second, that he feels only that the motion should be put to a vote — not necessarily that he is bound to vote for the motion. The appeal from the decision of the chair is essentially a motion to reverse the decision just announced. Thus, by its very nature, it is a motion with a negative effect, and as such is the reverse of almost every other motion. This creates some problems in putting the motion to a vote, because a "yes" vote on the appeal means that the voter wants to reverse rather than sustain the decision of the chairman. As the chairman asks for the vote, he should put the question in this way: "All those who would sustain the ruling of the chair, please say 'aye'! Those opposed, say 'nay.'" He should state the outcome and result of the vote, such as, "The 'aye's' have it. The decision of the chair is sustained, and discussion will proceed on the amendment which has been ruled germane."

DIVISION OF THE HOUSE

When the chairman announces the results of a voice vote or a show of hands vote which has not been literally counted, he is not really rendering a decision. He is reporting his judgment of the probable majority. Occasionally, he will be in doubt about which side actually did prevail. In such a case, he has only to say, "The chair is in doubt. Will those who are in favor of adopting the motion please stand. Those opposed." He will then announce the results of the votes counted.

When the chairman believes that one side or the other really did prevail, he announces the outcome of the vote. If at that time any member of the organization believes that the chairman has erred in his judgment of the majority, he may interrupt to say, "Mr. Chairman, I call for a division," or he may simply say, "division." At this point, without need for a second, the chairman proceeds to secure a count of those voting on each side of the issue and announces the result. A member may request a division any time between the moment that the question is put ("Are you ready to vote on the motion to contribute $10.00 from the treasury to the United Fund? Those who favor the motion . . .") and the moment that another motion is brought before the house.

The wording of the motion to divide the house follows a tradition dating to the early British Parliament, and which is still followed as votes are taken on important issues. In order to be sure that there was no mistake in the counting of votes and that no member's vote was overlooked or cast twice, the members of Parliament file out into one of two rooms — one for the "yes" vote and the other for the "nay" vote — and there are counted. This amounts to a literal "division of the house." It is not likely that the organizations of today have this kind of facilities, but the "division of the house" can be accomplished by an actual counting of the members, either by raising hands or standing, or, at times, by a roll call vote with each member casting his personal vote as his name is called. Usually, the purpose of the division can be accomplished by a count, and some organizations severely restrict or prohibit the use of the roll call vote because it is very time consuming. In large organizations the unrestricted use of the roll call vote can make it impossible to accomplish necessary business, and thus it becomes a weapon in the hands of a willful minority wanting to frustrate the majority. In such cases it is well to include the restrictions as a part of the by-laws or standing rules, or to establish the practice that the chairman may rule that a simple vote count will suffice, and even to rule that a division is unnecessary when a voice vote has appeared decisive, so that if his decision is appealed it will reliably be supported by a majority of the members.

WITHDRAWING OR MODIFYING A MOTION

The motion to withdraw or modify a main motion is often the easiest way to dispose of a motion that has served the purpose of bringing a subject before an organization for discussion, but has proven to be unpopular in its specific provisions or too vague. When either of these circumstances prevails — when it will take more procedural maneuvering to amend a motion than it would simply to back up a bit and take a new run at the topic — it is time to withdraw or modify the original motion and offer a new one. This motion is relatively common in organizations whose members are familiar with procedural rules, but often it gets bogged down in misunderstanding. One widely misunderstood factor about the motion to withdraw is what to do with it once it is proposed. Any member of the group can offer the motion to withdraw. It need not be either the person who proposed the motion or the person who seconded. This stems from the parliamentary fact that once a motion is made and seconded it is the property of the entire organization. It no longer "belongs" or is credited to the people who brought it before the group. For this reason, the chairman is not bound to inquire particularly of the maker or seconder of the motion about their preference in the matter. He simply asks for the common consent of the organization to withdraw or modify the motion. This requires unanimous action of the organization. The most likely sources of opposition do lie with the mover and seconder, so it is more a matter of courtesy and of assuring everyone that these two offer no more opposition than do any other members that might guide the chairman to ask them specifically if they have any objection. In the event that common consent is not forthcoming, the chairman puts the motion to withdraw to a vote, and a simple majority vote will withdraw a motion, irrespective of the way the mover and/or seconder vote. Were it not thus, a minority of one would be accorded more importance than the majority of the members in gross violation of the basic principles of parliamentary rule.

DIVISION OF A QUESTION

Often business will be brought before an organization in a form that lumps two or more separate matters together in the same motion. For instance, when a Resolutions Committee reports, its chairman will say "Mr. Chairman, I move the adoption of the following resolutions," and then may proceed to present any number of resolutions. One of the first formal actions taken by any organization — the adoption of a constitution — is another example. In these and other cases where the motion can be logically divided, it is possible that the complex motion might be jeopardized, because a few of the members object to each of the individual aspects of the proposal, though a majority favors the general idea. The cumulative effect of opposition to each of the parts could be the defeat of the entire motion. Just this situation prevailed for several sessions of the United States Congress regarding the bill to grant statehood to Alaska and Hawaii. By keeping the statehood proposal for the two territories under a single bill, the opposition to each was added together, and statehood was withheld from both. It was only when the two were presented as separate proposals that those who favored each had the opportunity to vote "aye" thereby extending statehood to the favorite.

Common sense would dictate that there ought to be a way to handle this kind of multi-faceted motion so that each successive aspect can be examined, and so that the total action on the motion will reflect the will of the majority — and there is just such a way: any member can move to divide the question, simply by saying "Mr. Chairman, I move to divide the question." This motion is decided by the chair asking for common consent of the members, specifying how the motion will be divided, or by ruling that the motion is not divisible. If there is objection to the chairman's decision he should treat the motion as any other motion, specifying the parts into which the main motion is to be divided, and putting the motion to divide to a vote of the members. A simple majority will then decide whether or not to divide the main motion.

OBJECTING TO CONSIDERATION

Occasionally a motion will be made that lies either beyond the limits of the competency of the organization or those of propriety. It is proper when such a motion is offered, before debate has begun (which means immediately following the restatement of the motion by the chairman, or during the first speaker's opening statement, before anyone else is recognized for the purpose of discussing the motion) to say, "Mr. Chairman, I move to object to consideration of the motion." Because the effect of this motion is to forestall any discussion of the main motion, it requires no second, but is put immediately to a vote, without discussion. If adopted by two-thirds majority, the main motion is put aside without any comment; if it fails to receive the necessary two-thirds majority, discussion may proceed on the main motion. This motion is rarely used, because few situations call for it. In most instances the impropriety of a motion would be a matter of form rather than substance. A member might move to change national policy respecting international affairs in an organization that has the power only to adopt a resolution expressing its viewpoint rather than directly effecting such a change. Three courses of action are possible at this point: a motion to amend would be in order, changing the original motion to conform to the powers of the organization; a motion to object to consideration would be a possibility, though perhaps no member would think of it, or if one did, not in time to gain recognition before discussion had begun, after which this motion cannot be properly offered; or one of the other incidental motions — the motion to withdraw the main motion — might be introduced.

Objecting to consideration of a motion is intended for those situations where the substance of a motion is such that it really demands not to be discussed. A motion which is embarrassing, malicious, ill-advised, or just stupid deserves to be cut off without discussion because the members should not be imposed upon to give it serious consideration. As the motion is stated or as the first contribution is made to a debate on the motion, it will become clear that discussion should be stopped before it gets started. That can best be accomplished by objecting to consideration.

UNDOING BUSINESS

You cannot unscramble an egg, but neither the person nor organization has yet existed which has not found it necessary to reverse or at least to re-examine a decision already made. For this reason provision has been made to bring business back to the floor of a meeting when there is good reason to believe that the initial decision might or should be reversed because of a change in the parliamentary situation.

Generally, such a change can be assumed when information not available when the motion was initially discussed becomes available, or when the voting membership present at the meeting has undergone some change (the presence of new members or the departure of some who were present). If the chairman feels there is no real possibility for a change in the outcome of a second consideration of a motion, he should refuse to permit renewed discussion of previous action.

Business is brought back before a meeting by one of two special forms of the main motion. The first and most direct motion is the motion to repeal (or rescind), which reverses the earlier action as it is adopted. The second is the motion to reconsider, which essentially turns back the clock to a moment or two before the vote was originally taken and permits further discussion and a second vote.

Repealing

When a member believes that he has due cause to propose that the organization reverse an earlier decision, he should offer the following motion after being recognized by the chairman:

MEMBER: I move to repeal the motion passed at our last meeting to hire a half-time secretary for our club.

Following a second, the discussion should focus on the continued desirability of the course of action earlier agreed upon. At the close of discussion, the chairman puts the question as follows:

CHAIRMAN: The question is on repeal of the motion to hire a half-time secretary for our club. This requires a two-thirds vote. All of those who favor the repeal raise your hands. Those opposed. The repeal carries. We shall not hire a half-time secretary for our club.

The requirement of a two-thirds majority to repeal previous action constitutes the most significant difference between the motion to repeal and the usual main motion. Because the nature of the motion is limited, it cannot be amended, since there is no way to amend without changing the effect which will be accomplished.

It could be argued that because an organization commits itself to a course of action through a simple majority vote, it should be able to reverse its decision with the same procedure. The danger in this view lies in the fact that most organizations transact their business with only a fraction of their membership present and voting at each meeting. The usual number necessary to conduct a regular meeting (the quorum) is seldom more than a simple majority, and in many cases it varies downward to ten or fifteen per cent, or just "those members present." It would be possible, then, for a proposal adopted by those present at one meeting to be repealed by an almost totally different group within the organization. This would lead to a very unstable situation with members and officers seldom sure that any actions taken by the group were sufficiently positive to warrant implementation. The requirement of a two-thirds majority provides a larger measure of stability, while allowing an organization to take a second look and, if necessary, reverse an unwise action.

There are circumstances under which past actions cannot be reversed. First, no organization can simply adopt a motion which intends to undo something which has already been done. Just as the egg cannot be unscrambled by a motion to repeal an earlier action, neither can anyone unwrite a letter to the congressman. Second, no organization can reverse the pledge of its word or a contract. For instance, the motion stated above — hiring a half-time secretary — could not be repealed if any negotiations had been entered into that obligated the club to hire someone. This limitation is enforceable in the courts if the commitment has led to some loss to the potential employee or constitutes a breach of contract.

Reconsidering

The second form in which past actions may be brought back to an organization for further debate is through the motion:

"Mr. Chairman, I move to reconsider the motion adopted earlier in this meeting to hire a half-time secretary for our club."

This particular form is less direct than the motion to repeal, but it has the advantage of being applicable to motions that have been defeated as well as those that have been adopted. Its use has been restricted to motions adopted or rejected earlier in the same meeting, or, in the instance of organizations that meet periodically for two or more days, to motions acted upon on the preceding day. These restrictions are intended to limit the possibility of arriving at a revote with a group which varies widely from those who voted initially. Thus, the vote on this motion takes a different approach to the possibility of shifting participants, and therefore it does not require a two-thirds majority to adopt. At least if the membership present has changed enough to alter the majority, they have done so within the same meeting and should know that actions taken are subject to reconsideration.

The motion to reconsider is intended primarily to accommodate that rather unusual instance when, after a motion has been discussed and acted upon, some additional information or viewpoint might cause further discussion to change the minds of some and hence change the outcome of the revote.

The rule books vary on one important restriction on the use of the motion to reconsider. Col. Robert and his direct followers require that the person who proposes the motion to reconsider must have voted on the prevailing side in the earlier action. Several modern authors note that because it has become common practice in most organizations to vote by voice or show of hands, without a precise count, it is difficult, if not impossible, to enforce this rule; so it should not be a stated requirement. Regardless of which view is held in any specific organization, the rationale is the same; the motion to reconsider should be in order only when there is a reasonable possibility that a revote would reverse an earlier action. When a member of the winning side moves to reconsider, it constitutes such a possibility. He and others might want to change their minds in view of new developments. On the other hand, it is perfectly possible for any member, seeing a majority vote developing, to cast his vote with those members solely in order to be eligible later to propose reconsideration when some of his friends are present. Requiring that the member who seeks to propose the motion has voted on the prevailing side is not an efficient safeguard. Perhaps the best way to protect the majority against the die-hard proponent of a rejected point of view is to permit the motion to reconsider to be made, and to call on its proponent for the first remarks to the members. If he does not establish the probability in the mind of the chairman that the vote will change the earlier action, the chairman can rule the motion out of order and proceed with the rest of the business at hand.

He should, of course, use discretion, bearing in mind that his decision can be appealed and balancing the possible expenditure of time against the need to assure full and fair consideration of substantive motions.

The motion to reconsider, in addition to restrictions on time when it is permissible and the need to establish the possibility of change, has factors that make it less efficient than the motion to repeal. Two votes are necessary to effect any change in the earlier voting. The first vote, on the motion to reconsider, simply turns back the clock to the moment before the vote was called and reopens discussion on the substantive motion. After continuing discussion until the new information has been introduced or the new voting members have had a chance to make up their minds, it is necessary to call another vote on the substantive motion itself. The whole affair is settled with a single vote when the question is on the motion to repeal.

SUMMARY

Among the useful motions encountered less frequently in formal parliamentary meetings than the substantive main motion and those motions that modify or delay action, are those motions designed to assure the rights of any individual member, to provide for an accurate count of the vote, to clarify the effect of a vote by separating independent aspects of multiple motions, to stop action on a motion by removing it from the floor or preventing its consideration, to recall past actions for reversal or reaffirmation and the motions to recess or adjourn. Each of these is designed to control procedure so that the meeting continues to move toward its avowed goals of abiding by the majority will while protecting the rights of each member.

Chapter 9

ORGANIZATIONAL AND PROCEDURAL STRUCTURE

Will Rogers is reputed to have said, "Just let six people get together with the same bias, and they will organize and start collecting dues." This observation of the American scene is not much of an overstatement. Almost every group, however small at the start and however limited or temporary its primary goal, establishes some basic written set of rules. Perhaps this is done as much because the American public has come to expect documents describing organizational and procedural structure as it is done for those within the group themselves. If we don't have a constitution, we are not, by definition, a club, a committee, or a "group." Even when no such document physically exists, certain individuals tend to see themselves as "members" of a group that meets repeatedly, and they behave as if there were a set of rules. After a time, when patterns have been set by tradition or repeated practice, they may be summarized in writing for the benefit of new members or in order to inform the outside public of the nature of the group.

"Constitution" may seem to be a very formal word to describe the organizational structure of some of the partly social, partly business groups in which we participate. In some instances the groups, seeking to avoid the formality of a "constitution," label their basic rules "by-laws"; others may call them "standing rules." At the other end of the formality line, some organizations have all three kinds of regulations, with a different way of amending each one. Whatever the label, the purpose and the content of each has the same elements.

The constitution of any organization sets forth those agreements that form the basis on which the group will operate. It states the group's purpose or goals and the structure and process through which it intends to work in order to achieve the goals. The basic document should have two characteristics: it should not contain too many details, and it should be difficult to change. If there are few details, there will be little need to amend the basic statement. If the constitution is made purposely difficult to alter, the group is more surely bound to stay close to its original purpose and to dissolve or re-group when the goal is achieved, or when efforts to achieve it are to be abandoned.

FORMING A NEW ORGANIZATION

One way to understand how any organization arrived at its present state is to review the usual way in which an organization is formed.

At some time, people wish to form an organization for the promotion or prevention of some activity or belief that is near to their heart. It is altogether possible that such an organization already exists someplace, but that need not prevent the establishment of another, and that after a time they may get together and form a new statewide, regional, or national superorganization. Forming an organization is quite simple. And the simpler it is kept, the more durable it is likely to be.

First, there must be people who agree that a new organization is desirable to make the initial plans. They should follow the suggestions in Chapter 2, "When to Hold a Meeting," as they bring together those whom they believe to be interested in the proposed group.

At the first meeting, one of the founders should call the group to order by rapping a gavel or clearly calling, "Will the group (or 'meeting') please come to order?" When order is established, he may proceed in one of two ways. He may assume that everyone expects to proceed in a traditional way and say, "I move that Mr. Warren Cushing act as temporary chairman. Is there a second to that motion? Will those in favor say 'aye'? Those opposed, 'no'? Will Mr. Cushing please take the chair?" This is a quick and efficient way of getting things started. It might, however, be so efficient that some of the group would resent the appearance of autocracy by those who made the original arrangements.

An alternative takes an additional step that would help those present to gather their thoughts and participate in another of the decisions that must be made. Instead of proceeding immediately to name temporary officers, the member might say, "I move that we proceed temporarily according to standard parliamentary practice. Is there a second? All in favor say, 'aye'? Those opposed say 'no'? The motion carries and this meeting will follow standard parliamentary procedure." Inasmuch as this is a procedural motion, and because there should be a certain momentum to get things under way, it is permissible to proceed to that vote without calling for discussion. At the same time, the very mention of parliamentary procedure is enough to arouse fears in some and a desire to demonstrate some knowledge on the part of others, so anyone might raise a point of information or seek recognition to discuss the implications of such a motion. The person who offers the motion must be prepared to handle this situation so that rights are acknowledged but the goal of setting up the initial structure is not unduly delayed. He might, therefore, respond to any attempts to gain recognition by saying, "At the moment we have no rules to govern ourselves. If you will wait until the meeting acts on this motion, our procedure will be determined, and your questions can be answered." He can then proceed to call for the vote on the motion having made clear why discussion is not desirable at that point.

After the motion has been adopted, the next few steps are determined by standard procedure. Step I is to name a temporary chairman, who will then assume the chair and proceed to Step II, which is to name a temporary secretary. In Step III the temporary chairman calls for the first business of the meeting, which is to entertain a motion that the meeting form a permanent organization for the purposes of . . . (whatever the general purposes were for calling the organizational meeting). Step IV is to appoint a committee to draw up a constitution. The person who called the meeting to order might well tell the members who are present just what those steps are, so they would be prepared to participate intelligently.

After specifying the three steps, the meeting has reached the point of naming the temporary chairman that was suggested as the first alternative. Depending on the size and nature of the group, the decision must be made either to propose a name agreed upon by the organizers of the meeting in advance or to open the meeting to suggestions from anyone present. If everyone attending is capable of performing well as chairman, there is no reason not to permit free choice. If there is a possibility that the job might go to someone who will not be an effective chairman, it is better to make a prior choice of the temporary chairman. Note that at this stage of organization the proper motion is "I move that _____ act as temporary chairman." This differs somewhat from the usual pattern of nominations by proposing a single candidate for acceptance or rejection instead of offering two or more candidates. In effect, then, it becomes a simple main motion. Because people are familiar with the standard form and voting procedures the meeting can move along comfortably.

When the temporary chairman has been named by a majority of those present and voting, he immediately takes the chair and says, "Is there a suggestion for temporary secretary?" The motion that a specific person act as temporary secretary is handled in the same way as the motion naming the temporary chairman. The person named assumes the job as secretary immediately upon election, and the initial structure is completed. The meeting is then prepared to consider the business for which it assembled. This has been cited as Step III above, and is the stage at which the meeting should be opened for discussion. Those who were instrumental in calling the organizational meeting should be given the opportunity to describe their ideas of the form and substance the group should assume. Others who are not so committed should ask questions and offer suggestions that will help to define the scope and purpose of the organization. Presumably, after some discussion of the motion to form a permanent organization, the meeting will adopt the motion, setting the stage for the next step in the organizational meeting.

The traditional meaning inherent in the motion to form a permanent organization is that there should be a constitution that defines the purposes and the structure of the organization. Such a "permanent" organization may well have a purpose that limits its life either in terms of time or goals. A "Committee to elect Kalb in 1970," for instance, should be dissolved or at least reconstituted following the 1970 elections. The National Polio Foundation, which carries on the "March of Dimes" campaigns, found itself out of a specific cause when the Salk vaccine brought polio under control. Through some interpretation of its constitution (and without undergoing the added legal maneuvers of changing its corporate structure) the Foundation has continued to exist and has extended its endeavors to support research on other childhood diseases.

The next step, then, is to provide for the creation of a constitution. Any member may propose, "I move that the chairman appoint a committee of three to draft a constitution for this organization and to report at the next meeting." Following the adoption of this motion, the chairman should announce the names of the individuals he is appointing, asking the consent of the members as follows: "If there is no objection, the chairman appoints Mr. Secord, Mr. Tutweiler, and Mr. Williamson as a committee to draft a proposed constitution and to report at our next meeting."

Finally, the meeting can adjourn — but this is one of those rare instances when no provision has been made for a later meeting, so it must not adjourn without specifying a time and place for a later meeting. The time lapse before the second meeting must give the constitutional committee time to do its job, but not be so long that the interest of the members will wane. It should conform as nearly as possible to the time and place of the first meeting, on the assumption that people at the first meeting would find that hour and place generally convenient later.

The temporary chairman calls the second meeting to order at the time and place decided at the organizational meeting. He then asks that the temporary secretary read the minutes of the organizational meeting. These are subjected to the approval of the members by the chairman, who says, "Are there any additions or corrections to the minutes? (PAUSE) None appearing, the minutes stand approved as read."

The first order of business following approval of the minutes is the report of the constitutional committee. The temporary chairman may either call on the chairman of that committee who should say, "Mr. Chairman, I move the adoption of the following constitution," or the temporary chairman may simply announce that "The motion before the house is on the adoption of the constitution to be read by the chairman of the constitution committee. Will the chairman please read the first article?"

It is a great help if the constitutional committee can provide each member written copies of the proposed constitution. If these are distributed to the members with the reminder of the meeting they have the opportunity to study the entire proposal, thereby making consideration of the document more effective. The usual procedure is to read each article, permitting discussion and possible amendment after each one. After every article is considered separately, discussion is permitted on the entire constitution, amendments are considered, and the question is then put on the original motion to adopt the constitution. When a majority votes in favor of the constitution, it takes effect immediately.

The only remaining step in implementing the constitution is election of officers in the manner prescribed by the constitution. The temporary chairman presides over the election of the senior officer, who takes the chair immediately following his election. The temporary secretary serves until the election of a successor who then assumes the job of recording minutes. Other officers also take office as elected, though they may have no immediate assignment. If any formal oath or installation is prescribed, this should be performed. When election and installation is completed, the organization is fully established and prepared to do business.

THE CONSTITUTION

The basic structure of any organization of people joining together to achieve a common goal is very similar to the basic structure of any other group with a similar purpose. One may differ from another in a number of specific details, just as each person is unique, but when the details are removed they usually reveal a common skeletal structure. This organizational skeleton is the constitution. The goal of every constitutional committee should be to determine the minimum essentials that will provide the framework necessary to accomplish the purpose of the group and to state these essentials clearly and briefly. Details should be left to other documents or to the slow process of tradition. It is the responsibility of the constitutional committee to state only those ideas that establish an identity and a procedural basis on which the organization can begin to function. The constitution is the written contract between the members, stating mutual obligations and rights.

The precise format varies somewhat from one constitution to another with respect to the sequence of items, but the same essential factors appear in almost all. Articles I and II state the name and the purpose of the organization. Article III usually specifies qualifications and types of membership. Article IV names the officers and their terms of office. Regular and special meetings are prescribed by Article V. The parliamentary authority that will govern all situations not specifically provided for by the organization itself is named in Article VI, and the process of amending the constitution is specified in Article VII. All these provisions are necessary, for if any one is omitted, the organization lacks a vital element. There is little sense to an organization without a defined purpose. Without membership there is no organization; without officers there is no structure; and without meetings there is no chance for collective action and no need for structure. Some might argue that there need not be a citation of parliamentary authority because each group can generate its own rules. On the other hand, it is pointless to ignore all previous experience and very nearly impossible to anticipate all possible situations that might develop in an organization's lifetime. Providing a basis for the development of individual rules is wise, if not absolutely essential. And finally, even the most confident of constitutional committees would acknowledge that sometime in the indeterminate future there might be a need to change the constitution in some way, so provision to make change possible must be made.

The job of the constitutional committee can be made much easier if it recognizes the fact that these minimum essentials are common to all constitutions and that its function is to set them forth so that they identify the organization and provide means for its operation. This means that they can follow the pattern set by a similar organization, rewording the specific articles to suit their own purposes. A sample constitution is included here to facilitate the organization of a society for the study and practice of meeting management.

Article I — Name
The name of this organization is the Q.E.D. Meeting Management Society.

Article II — Purpose
The purpose of this organization is to enhance the knowledge, understanding, and skill of its members in order that they participate more effectively in the management of meetings conducted according to parliamentary rules and traditions.

Article III — Membership
Any person subscribing to the purposes of this organization may become an active member by being present and voting on the adoption of this constitution or upon nomination by an active member and election by a majority of those voting at a regular meeting.

Article IV — Officers
Section One. The officers of this organization are a president, vice-president, secretary, and parliamentarian. Their duties are those usually associated with those offices.

Section Two. After the initial election to fill each of the offices, a secretary will be elected at each alternate meeting, who will then succeed to the office of vice-president, president, and parliamentarian at the beginning of the meeting following each successive election. No person will be re-elected to office until all members have served.

Section Three. The elected officers constitute an executive committee to plan meetings and act for the society during the intervals between meetings.

Article V — Meetings
Section One. Regular meetings will be held weekly during a regular class period when the university is in session.

Section Two. Special meetings may be called by the executive committee, and must be called upon written request of one-fourth of the members.

Section Three. A quorum for any meeting will consist of a majority of the membership.

Article VI — Parliamentary Authority
In all matters not covered by its constitution and by-laws this organization will be governed by the *Sturgis Standard Code of Parlia-*

mentary Procedure. (Any standard procedural authority may be specified here.)

Article VII — Amendments

This constitution may be amended at any regular meeting by a two-thirds vote, provided that due notice has been given at the preceding regular meeting.

BY-LAWS

When a skeletal constitution is adopted, there is often a need for providing more detail in another parallel document. This need not be done immediately. As the organization discovers certain practices that are convenient or necessary are not provided in the constitution or in the parliamentary authority, they can be adopted as by-laws. Membership dues is an example of a provision that might well be specified as a by-law. Costs and activities may fluctuate enough to demand rather frequent changes in dues. An increase in dues should not be possible without some prior notification, but a dues change is not so basic to the operations of the organization that it needs the same consideration as a constitutional amendment. For this reason an intermediate requirement might be specified for amending the by-laws, such as adoption by a majority vote, following notice at the previous regular meeting.

Other structural elements that might be included in the by-laws are: standing committees, method of nominating and electing officers, any special duties or powers of officers, and the procedure for amending by-laws.

ORDER OF BUSINESS

One aspect of parliamentary tradition which has grown to be both an asset and a liability is the "order of business." It is an asset because it prescribes a routine that lets members know the sequence of items. At the same time, the "order of business" may become a liability if the members treat the contents of the routine matters as unimportant items — something that happens every meeting; therefore, they need not pay attention. This view belies the reasoning behind the routine.

The traditional order of business following the call to order is as follows:

1. Reading of the minutes of the previous meeting, and their approval
2. Reports of standing committees

3. Reports of special committees
4. Unfinished business
5. New business

The Minutes

Mention was made in Chapter 6 of the importance of the minutes in recording actions taken by an organization. It is important that the record of past actions be accurately kept because the organization is liable for any commitments that are recorded in the minutes. It is theoretically possible that an unscrupulous secretary might include an item which said, "It was moved and seconded that the secretary be paid a salary of $100 per month; the motion passed," when no such motion had been made. If all of the members were not actively listening to the reading of the minutes, and they were approved, the secretary could sue for the salary and win the case in court. Perhaps most secretaries are honest, but participants in meetings might listen more actively to see that the minutes report business accurately. Likewise, an effective chairman should not permit conversations among neighbors to interrupt the reading of the minutes.

Questions are often raised concerning the form that minutes should take: should the names of those who made or seconded motions be included; should a summary of the discussion be included; what about points of order and points of information? Minutes should be a record of all motions acted upon by the organization. As long as this minimum is met, a rather wide latitude is permissible. Different organizations follow different patterns. It is not legally necessary to record the names of those who propose motions, though some organizations prefer to do so. If minutes are distributed to people who have not attended a meeting, or if meetings are held only once a year, it may be wise to include a summary of the discussion on a motion. Unless the chairman's ruling on a point of order is appealed, leading to a vote by the members, there is no compelling reason to include it in the minutes, though it is not altogether improper.

Whenever possible, it is a good practice to include a copy of the minutes with the notice of the next meeting. This will help members to prepare for it and will save the time of reading minutes as a meeting starts. When minutes have been distributed, the chairman will say, "The minutes have been distributed. Are there any additions or corrections? (PAUSE) None appearing, the minutes stand approved as distributed." If a member notes a necessary correction, the chairman will say, "The minutes will stand approved as corrected."

Reports of Committees

There is nothing more deadening to the interest and enthusiasm of the beginning of a meeting than the following dialogue:

CHAIRMAN: We are now ready for the committee reports. First, the standing committee on finance. Mr. Stone, will you report for your committee?

STONE: Mr. Chairman, there is nothing to report.

CHAIRMAN: Thank you. Will its chairman, Mr. Abernathy, report for the standing committee on publications?

ABERNATHY: We have no report, Mr. Chairman.

CHAIRMAN: Thank you. (etc. through several more standing and special committees.)

Even more important than loss of interest is the fact that this waste of time could be easily avoided by requesting that each committee chairman notify the presiding officer before the meeting starts if he has something to report. In this way the responsibility is placed on the person who has something to say. If he fails to make his place on the agenda, he can easily seek recognition and make his report, even if it comes later than its usual position in the meeting.

Because committee reports may fall into either of two categories (information or action), as discussed in Chapter 5, the chairman of the committee can clarify the proper action to be taken by the organization by proposing the proper motion, either at the outset or the close of his report. He might say:

MR. CHAIRMAN, I move the adoption of the following report. (He then proceeds to read the report recommending a specification without waiting for a second, because the report carries the implicit endorsement of more than one member.)

or he might say:

(Following the reading of an information report) Mr. Chairman, I move that this report be received and filed.

When the committee chairman fails to offer the appropriate motion, the chairman may simply put the question of adopting the report to discussion and a vote, or he may propose that a report be received by common consent.

Unfinished Business

Any item of business that has been considered at an earlier meeting falls into the category of unfinished business if no final action was taken or if it can legitimately be brought back for repeal or reconsideration. This includes motions referred to committee (often action reports by committees are held for consideration here), postponed until this meeting, tabled, or pending when the previous meeting was adjourned, as well as motions adopted but not implemented, and therefore subject to repeal. One of the important functions of the minutes of previous meetings is to recall such items so that they are not simply left hanging. The secretary should maintain a list of such motions and supply a copy to the chairman, who may (but is not obliged to) remind the members of these items.

New Business

This portion of a meeting may prove either to be the most enthusiastic or the briefest of all. If the members are interested in the purposes of the organization, it is probable that they will contribute some new ideas. An agenda committee may even have prepared a list of proposals to be considered. New ideas usually inspire the questions and comments that make for lively discussion. On the other hand, if the pace of the meeting prior to this point has been dull and slow, and the members are feeling the press of their next commitment, "new business" may well be an empty category.

The secretary can help by reminding the chairman of any impending events or necessary decisions, and the chairman may list one or more important items to remind the members of priority considerations.

SUMMARY

The constitution forms the frame upon which organizations develop. The process of forming a new organization is largely concerned with constructing a constitution that will state clearly and concisely the organization's purposes and procedural framework. The committee charged with drafting a constitution will find its job easier if they find and follow a prototype from a similar organization. By-laws may be added from time to time to spell out details of procedure or structure that will make the business run more smoothly. These should be less difficult to amend than the constitution, but they require more than the simple majority necessary to adopt ordinary motions.

Effort should be directed at promoting active attention to the items appearing regularly in the usual "order of business." If the members do not listen carefully during the early part of the meeting, the chances are that they will not be greatly interested in the rest of the business.

Repeated practice of proper procedure is the best means of gaining confidence and effectiveness in participating and leading business meetings of any size. If a meeting — however small or large, informal or formal — is to be operated democratically, each member, from the least experienced to the chairman, should be able to contribute to the management of the meeting. Therefore, each member must know as much as possible about the patterns, rules, procedures, and substantive matters. This knowledge grows with each meeting.

Chapter 10

STRATEGY
IN MEETING
MANAGEMENT

A meeting of people who share membership in an organization is akin to a sports event — a baseball game, football, basketball, or any other team sport. It progresses through a competition of ideas, introduced within a system of rules, toward the satisfaction of player-spectators as it achieves the goals of the group by determining the best available decisions. The better the players understand why the rules exist, the more skilled they become in performing within the rules and the more progress is made without delays due to infractions. There are no penalty boxes nor free throws in meetings, but the penalty of loss of time is very much akin to the loss of yardage in football. It is not enough to have a chairman who knows the rules and the means of expediting the organizational business. Every member will increase his own satisfaction and the efficiency and effectiveness of the entire organization as he becomes more knowledgeable about how to play the game without delaying it through rule infractions.

The competition of ideas effectively defines and clarifies the alternative solutions. The entire group of player-spectators gains not only through the satisfaction of participating in an effective game, but through the enactment of intelligent policies and plans developed by this collective problem-solving process. The best possible solution is, almost by definition, the plan or course of action agreed to by a majority of those voting after a consideration of alternatives.

The only way to achieve this "best possible solution" is to be thoroughly acquainted with the attributes of the action that you, as a member, favor. You should be equally well prepared to advance that action to a majority of the members both through persuasion and effective use of the parliamentary processes and should be aware of the potential arguments and countermoves that may be used by supporters of competing courses of action.

A knowledge of the attributes of the preferred course of action depends upon a thorough analysis of the problem confronting the organization, a determination of the criteria by which the acceptability of any proposal ought to be judged, and the creation of a proposal that will provide more new advantages than problems. When confronted with a limitation on action because of the organization's constitution or by-laws, for instance, there are certain aspects of the problem that can be determined immediately by asking a few questions. "Are we faced with a constitutional prohibition, a vague statement, or a lack of any provision at all?" Answers to this question will suggest the nature of the remedy. Next, perhaps, might be an inquiry into the cause of the present status of the constitution: if there is a prohibition, "Why was this included?"; if there is a vague statement, "Why was this provision left unclear? Have circumstances changed since the constitution was written? Was this provision, perhaps, left purposefully vague to permit but not encourage this action?" If the document is altogether silent on the point, one might ask "Why? Was this possibility not foreseen? Was it considered outside the scope of interest for the organization? Ought we now consider this action?" Answers to these and similar analytical questions will provide both a solid understanding of the proposal and a means of supporting its adoption.

As a motion is presented for adoption, the usual pattern is that the person who presents the motion speaks first in its support. After it is moved, seconded, and then stated by the chairman, the chairman will usually first recognize the member who made the motion. If the mover does not want to speak himself, he at least has the option of designating who will lead the support for the motion. The assumption is, of course, that the person who offers the motion has done the most thinking about it and is thus in the best position to explain his reasoning to the rest of the members. To be persuasive, the explanation of the motion should highlight the supporting answers to the questions that guide the analysis of the problem. Those questions that indicate only the blind alleys and negative answers should be omitted, and those questions that lead directly toward the action proposed should be emphasized so that maximum agreement can be attained at each step of the explanation. If the motion can be closely allied with the value systems of the members, its adoption is promoted. This concern for the values of the members spans the distance between the desire for leisure and personal enjoyment called into play by support of the motion to sponsor a dance, to the social value of belief in hard work and in enduring some discomfort for a worthwhile cause that can arouse support for a car-wash project to raise money for a favored charity. In any instance, the more closely the motion is allied with goals held desirable by the members, the more probable is its adoption.

Equally important with the need to link substantive motions affirmatively with the members' values is the need to introduce the proposal so as to arouse the least possible amount of legalistic or procedural opposition. For instance, the person who wants to obligate his organization to contribute to the local United Fund should propose this as a separate main motion, not as an amendment to the committee motion to adopt a proposed budget. In this latter case, the substance of the proposal becomes mixed up with the main motion, some of the members may be confused by the process or the possible motive, and the issue is less clearly drawn than when it is brought to the floor as a separate and distinct motion. When a proposal does appear in an unusual form the members naturally wonder why. Two obvious answers usually result: the sponsor of the idea may not have fully planned his motion and had to work it in as best he could; or the sponsor of the idea is not sure that the proposal could stand on its own merits, so he is trying to gain its adoption by allying it with a proposal that seems likely to be adopted even if combined with the questionable proposal. Either of these judgments could defeat even a highly warranted proposal, so it behooves the proponent to avoid the suspicion that attaches to an unusual parliamentary maneuver. When the substance of a motion is subject to the judgment of the peculiar means of proposing it, the decision is based more on the legal technicalities than on the merits of the case. This happens when an indictment is improperly drawn and the court decides on that basis, not on the guilt or innocence of the accused person.

Because parliamentary debate is intended to continue so long as there is a desire to express opinion on both sides of a proposition, it is necessary for supporters of a motion to assess and anticipate the opposition's potential. Even the most informal of meetings will profit from the practice of alternating speakers who favor adoption of a motion with those who oppose it. The chairman can easily start by recognizing the member who proposed the motion, then an opponent, a supporter, an opponent, etc. When there is no one left to speak on one side or the other, it can be assumed that a majority of the members are ready to vote. It does not necessarily mean that all possible arguments for either side have been advanced, nor that the side that first ran out of prospective speakers will lose. It simply gives the chairman an opportunity to seek common consent to stop debate and proceed to vote. If his request gives rise to further last-minute statements, this need not bother anyone. Even the suggestion tends to move the organization closer to a vote.

As a member plans his defense, he has two general classifications of offensive positions to explore and anticipate. The first is the substantive defense of the motion: when a motion to have a picnic is offered, the member who proposes it must be prepared to defend the idea against alternatives such as a dinner party, dance, or potluck supper. He may have to support the particular day against alternatives. There can be any number of other alternatives, depending on how complex the main motion is. The second area of defense lies in making sure that the member knows the possible ways of disposing of the motion other than direct adoption. He should know how far he is prepared to go to insure at least fair consideration, rather than seeing his motion defeated on procedural grounds rather than on the merits of the proposal. At times it is advisable to permit and even encourage one or another of the delaying subsidiary motions because they might insure better understanding of the motion or might delay final action until a later meeting when more support might be mustered. These are decisions that the proponent of action must be prepared to make on the spot, having previously determined the criteria on which to base the decision. If it seems that a motion has a good chance of success and that its passage would benefit the entire organization, it is wise to do the best possible job of fighting off all subsidiary motions, except that of voting immediately, when it seems that all those who so wish have had their say. This sort of action often forestalls a needless postponement of an action that most favor, but fear to seem to be too eager for its immediate enactment.

In certain circumstances a compromise, either substantive or procedural, may offer the best line of defense. Again, the decision of when to defend and when to compromise must be made on the basis of an immediate estimate of the pressures and the odds favoring adoption. It helps to have considered the alternatives — what reaction to adopt in the face of each possible proposal for change. When this has been done, one often can make a small change and gain much support for the principle involved in the main motion. Skill in this type of parliamentary maneuvering comes mainly from experience rather than study. Reading and participating in some study and testing the responses of people is a means of enhancing one's ability to respond to the situation with speed and confidence. The story has often been told that Sir Winston Churchill worked long and hard, not only over his early speeches in Parliament, but also in anticipating opposition arguments and creating ready replies. This effort paid double for Churchill, who was thus able not only to control his tendency to stutter, but to overpower his opposition with counterargument.

In one sense, the initial acceptance of parliamentary rules constitutes the initial compromise. Each person agrees in advance that his rights and responsibilities will be equal with those of the others. Within that framework, then, lies ample room for further compromise in the interests of creating and sustaining harmonious group relations and effective member participation.

SUMMARY

In sum, effective parliamentary policy and strategy consist of a thoughtful assessment by each member of what he feels that organization ought to do, a consideration of the best way to get the members of the organization to commit themselves to that goal, and an application of the most clear and direct means of achieving that commitment.

Chapter 11

LEARNING MEETING MANAGEMENT

A precise student of homilies once commented that *"All* practice makes permanent; only *good* practice makes *perfect."* And so it is with meeting management. Study of the philosophy, the fundamentals, and even the language of managing meetings will contribute only a limited amount toward the goal of effective participation and leadership in meetings. The next necessary step is to put the philosophy, the fundamentals, and the language into practice in order to see how they really work and to develop a feeling of being comfortable in a meeting. Some of the phrases, such as "Mr. Chairman, I move that . . .," are not part of our everyday conversation. In a business meeting, and even occasionally in a committee, we talk in a new language that is not quite so "foreign" as French, but is no easier to use until the sounds and the meanings become part of our thinking.

The process of learning meeting management, then, is largely one of practice — *good* practice — in as many situations as can be devised. This means that the learning can go on — and *must* go on — both in and out of class when the primary purpose is learning the rules, and when the primary purpose is committing an organization to action. Just as the fraternity that seeks to educate its members to some of the social graces requires suit coats, ties, and polite behavior at the dinner table, and the foreign-language institute requires that participants speak only the language being learned, the way to develop confidence and effectiveness in meetings is to take part in meetings.

WITH OTHER CLASS OBJECTIVES

When your study of meeting management is a part of learning more about all kinds of speaking situations, it is possible to organize a number of classroom activities that integrate some of the language and procedures of meetings with other assignments.

1. A chairman can be appointed for the initial round of speeches in the public speaking or the fundamentals class, where members introduce each other. When he is furnished with a seating chart that identifies the members, a member could rise, address the chair ("Mr. Chairman"), be recognized, ("Mr. Walker"), state his purpose in seeking recognition ("Mr. Chairman, I would like to introduce Mr. Johnson."), receives permission ("You may proceed with your introduction."), and begin his introduction with an acknowledgment that his remarks in this formal situation are addressed to the chairman ("Mr. Chairman and members of the class, I would like you to know. . . .").

A similar pattern of appointing a student chairman to preside over class meetings on the days of speaking assignments can be followed throughout the course, whether the speaking order is pre-established or voluntary. Each instance where a student has the opportunity to acknowledge an introduction makes him more comfortable saying "Thank you, Mr. Chairman."

2. Exercises in public speaking are often arranged so that several speakers present different aspects of the same problem in a series of speeches on the same day, in a symposium or a debate. It is almost inevitable that such programs have a chairman, and, as time permits following the series of talks, provision usually is made for a forum period in which the other members of the class have the opportunity to ask questions and to offer their own points of view. These programs are special types of meetings that vary only slightly from the investigative meetings of committees and the decision-making meetings of the parent organizations.

The functions exercised by the chairman are those of the formal business meeting. The function of the speakers and the other members of the class is identical with their function in a business meeting entertaining a committee report that is divded among members of the committee, or that through the submission of a minority report presents two sides as in a debate. Practice in organizing and delivering the brief, cogent, and clear talk that explains a situation or sets forth a point of view is practice in the kind of talk that is most effective in the business meeting. Likewise, practice in listening to a speaker, analyzing what he says, and framing a question for clarification or a hostile question aimed at exposing a weakness in his evidence or argument is practice for effective participation in a business meeting.

3. Courses which include assignments using problem-solving group discussion are by their very nature offering practice in the business

of committee operation. Such assignments can be made most directly valuable to learning meeting management by requiring a written report summarizing the information and/or recommendations agreed to by the group (committee). Practice in presenting oral reports of committee activities can be gained by coordinating this type of assignment with the symposium or debate-forum described above.

4. The characteristics of a well-worded parliamentary motion are inherent in a well-worded topic sentence for a talk. Each should be brief, clear, simple, and complete. The distinction between the two arises in the words that preface the substance of the sentence: "I move. . . ." As the student realizes that his efforts to develop proficiency in creating an effective topic sentence for a talk will also be useful to him in phrasing a proper motion, and vice versa, he will be more motivated in his efforts.

The above suggestions start with the premise that practice in some aspect of meeting management can be easily integrated with activities designed primarily to develop skills useful in all types of oral communication situations. To a degree, then, it follows that any increase in the understanding and skills of oral communication will enhance effectiveness as a participant or a leader in a meeting. It does *not* follow, however, that the most effective development of proficiency in meeting management occurs when the learner is placing all of his concentration on the development of general communicative skills. Unless the classroom public speaking and discussion situations are structured to parallel the parliamentary situation, much of the opportunity to develop conscious experience in meeting management will be lost. On the other hand, in classroom study that is to include some consideration of parliamentary procedure (a "unit" of several days or weeks focusing directly on behavior during meetings) an early and repeated exposure to some of the routine elements of meetings will make the practice business meeting less uncomfortable for the students because they will be more familiar with many of its characteristics.

AS THE MAJOR CLASS OBJECTIVE

Direct classroom study of meeting management occurs in a wide range of situations including the junior high or high school civics class, the college or university fundamentals or public speaking class and the separate quarter or semester course, the non-credit continuing education workshop, the fee course offered by the professional parliamentarian or proficient amateur, and individuals who enroll themselves or are sponsored by clubs and organizations that see the need for more information and experience. Throughout this range of teachers and learners the universally accepted method of study is to establish an organization for the major purpose of learning more about how to participate more effectively in meetings. Just as the "investment clubs" learn about the operations of the stock market by pooling their financial resources and actually investing in stocks, the "parliamentary clubs" gain their skill by doing and studying how to do things best while they are participating. Likewise, as the "investment clubs" sometimes make a profit, the "parliamentary clubs" sometimes adopt motions or resolutions that create community action as a by-product rather than as an end in itself.

The best approach to establishing an organization serving as a vehicle for learning meeting management is to gain some practice in the fundamental procedures while studying the philosophy on which our meetings rest. This leads to the development of the structure for the organization, its adoption, and implementation.

Exercise 1 — Stating Main Motions. Each member of the class should write ten main motions, including motions to propose direct action, to recommend action, to request (petition) action, and to express a collective viewpoint (resolution). These will be evaluated by class members and the instructor for brevity, clarity, simplicity, and conciseness.

Exercise 2 — Presenting Main Motions. Permitting each class member to serve as chairman successively, the routine dialogue for presenting main motions should be practiced until it becomes comfortable for both member and chairman alike. Motions written for the first exercise can be used, and the following pattern used:

CHAIRMAN: The floor is open for new business.

MEMBER: Mr. Chairman (or Madam Chairman).

CHAIRMAN: Mr. Griffith.

GRIFFITH: I move (that, or to) . . .

OTHER MEMBER (without waiting for recognition): I second the motion.

CHAIRMAN: It has been moved and seconded (that, or to). . . . We shall dispense with discussion on the motion. Those who favor the motion say "aye." Those opposed, say "no." (Or a show of hands vote may be called for.) The motion is carried (or lost).

After the decision is announced, the chairman retires and his successor reopens the meeting for the next item of new business. By the time each member of the class has served as chairman several times and observed the process a number of times, the routine becomes well established. This exercise can be extended through more than one period and alternated with lecture or discussion.

Exercise 3 — Discussion and Debate on Motions. This was described in item 2 above. Any combination of brief talks relating to a main motion — ranging from a supporting talk of three to five minutes, followed by a single opposing speech and a one-minute rejoinder by the initiator of the motion, to unlimited questioning and debate — will provide experience for participants and chairman.

Exercise 4 — Amendments. After some confidence is gained in debating the main motion, amendments may be permitted. Important factors here include: (a) clear statement of intent (i.e., to strike, to add, to substitute), (b) clear restatement by the chairman so that members know how the motion would read if amended, (c) focus of debate on the amendment rather than on the main motion, (d) a clear vote on the amendment and announcement of decision, (e) debate continuing on the main motion as amended or not. As the process becomes familiar, questions of germaneness, the hostile amendment, amendment to an amendment should be raised.

Exercise 5 — Motions to Defer Action and Close Debate. To observe the effects of increasing the complexity by adding more possibilities and raising the question of precedence, use of the motions to postpone indefinitely, to refer to a committee, to postpone definitely, to lay on the table, and to close debate should be practiced.

The class will now have had some experience in using all of the most frequently used motions (except, perhaps for the point of order and point of information) and can easily and profitably take the steps necessary to establish a temporary, and then a permanent, organization. It will use a committee to draft and present a proposed constitution, adopt the constitution, and continue to operate as an organization to provide the additional experience possible within the limits of time. This will provide an opportunity to study and use the less frequent motions. Various rule books can be explored for differing provisions. Confidence and breadth of understanding of the ways and means of managing meetings of all degrees of formality will be increased. The factors of size, degree of unanimity, knowledge of procedural rules, and purpose of the meeting will become effective guides to good practice.

INDEPENDENT OBSERVATION AND STUDY

The study of meeting management is neither limited to the classroom nor dependent on participation in a group devoted to that purpose. Every individual who wants to increase his own knowledge and skill can spend whatever time he has available observing meetings and reading.

Observation

1. Begin with the meetings you normally attend. In addition to paying attention to the subjects being discussed, observe the determinants of appropriate formality (size, unanimity, knowledge of procedure, and purpose) and assess how well the meeting is progressing. Note the frequency with which various motions are used. Note the manner of taking action (common consent, voice vote, etc.), the way in which actions are recorded (minutes), the manner of participation of the chairman and participants.

2. Attend an open meeting of an organization of which you are not a member — a religious youth or adult group, a political organization, a campus or community interest club (Sailing or Outing Club, International Club, County Historical Society, P.T.A., etc.) and observe the same items. Compare your observations with those for your own organizations. Are there differences? Can you explain them? Which organization does the better job of meeting management? In what way? Why? What are the ways in which *you* (as a member or an officer) can improve your organization?

3. Attend an open meeting of a governing body (student senate, city council, school board, university or faculty senate, state or national legislature, etc.) observing the procedure which they follow. Compare this meeting with the others. Identify the differences and see if you can identify the sources of difference (in law, as a part of tradition, or any unique factors).

4. Attend and observe open committee meetings, hearings, or investigations connected with the above organizations. How do these differ from the business meetings? Do committees with similar purposes differ as much as their parent organizations?

Individual observation is a useful supplement to classroom study and can be made the subject of written and oral reports and discussion. At the same time, it is a valuable method of increasing awareness of the problems and solutions in the varied situations encountered in meetings.

Study

Reading a parliamentary rule book is rather like reading an encyclopedia — there is a good deal of interesting material, but the plot doesn't seem to hold together very well. The reader must supply most of the scene in order for the dialogue to come alive. The best time to read about how to manage a meeting is soon after attending a meeting. Situations are fresh in your mind. There may be some questions about whether or not things were done right. These questions will motivate and direct your reading. You may have to search two or more sources to prove to yourself whether or not an action was "right." It is possible to find conflict between (or even within) authorities, and this can raise further questions for further reading.

Every library will have a copy of Henry M. Robert's *Rules of Order Revised*, Seventy-fifth Anniversary Edition (Chicago: Scott, Foresman and Co., 1951). If it cannot be located, its loss can doubtless be attributed to its small size and large demand as the standard code cited in the constitutions of most American organizations. Alice F. Sturgis' *Standard Code of Parliamentary Procedure*, (New York: McGraw-Hill Book Co., 1950), is a similar authority, better adapted to reading and emergency consultation. State legislatures and the federal Congress publish rules for each session of each governing body including whatever rule revisions have been adopted as the session opens and organizes itself. Occasionally there will be comment in the current press about controversy over rule changes, such as the United States Senate rule providing for cloture (closing debate, or "anti-filibuster" rule).

Each permanent organization has its own written document that will provide information about how its meetings should be managed, and which every member *should* re-read periodically. Similarities and differences between these documents can provide stimulating questions and enlightening answers to the student of meeting management.

Textbooks and periodical articles describing participation and leadership in committees are available in great numbers. They vary widely in emphasis in a number of dimensions, such as style of leadership, purpose or goal of the committee, power to act and responsibility to other larger bodies.

SUMMARY

The viewpoint of this book has been that the range and scope of meeting management is broad; that the principles and practices applying to people working together to solve a problem are based on everyday conversational good manners and differ with size, unanimity or hostility, sophistication or knowledge of certain forms and formalities, and the particular purpose or goal of the group. These are the subjects of the study of meeting management. Sources which develop sensitivity to people and problems, and suggest ways to act and react constructively, are the proper subjects of study.

MEETING MANAGEMENT CHART

All motions require a second. Motions take precedence over (are in order when) those listed below them are pending° (except indefinite postponement — not in order when an amendment is pending).

Adjourn	*Not* Debatable	Majority
Recess	Debate on Length	Majority
(Object to Consideration)	*Not* Debatable	2/3
Close Debate	*Not* Debatable	2/3
Limit Debate	Debate only on time permitted	2/3

Defer Action

Lay on Table	*Not* Debatable	Majority
Postpone Definitely	Debate on how long to postpone	Majority
Refer to Committee	Debate on merit of referral	Majority
Postpone Indefinitely°	Debatable	Majority

Substantive

Amend	Debatable	Majority
MAIN MOTION	Debatable	Majority
Reconsider	Debatable	Majority
Repeal	Debatable	2/3

For Immediate Action by Chairman, without a second, debate, or vote (may interrupt when necessary):

Immediate Needs

Request for Information
Parliamentary Inquiry
Point of Order
Division of the House
Withdraw a Motion
Division of a Question

Control Chairman

APPEAL from the decision of the Chair

Requires a Second
Is Debatable
Majority Vote Carries

INDEX

DATE DUE